Chaos In Satan's Garden

A Novel By:

Mustafa Alqorna

ISBN: 978-1-954297-89-0

Alpha Book Publisher
www.alphapublisher.com

Ordering Information:
Quantity sales. Special discounts are available on quantity purchases by corporations, associations, and others. For details, contact the publisher at the address above.
For orders by U.S. trade bookstores and wholesalers, visit www.alphapublisher.com/contact-us to learn more.

Printed in the United States of America

Table of Contents

Dedication

To all the detainees who dream of freedom.

Mustafa Alqorna

Chapter 1.

So wretched I was when I boarded the plane from Al-Smara Elementary School to Cuba in one go. A short while ago, people were ululating as if we were heading to paradise. My mother was crying oddly, which worried me, and my father was unhappy. It was a comic game that would not end peacefully. I thought to myself, it would be better if I stayed in the Sahara with my uncle.

We came to the Sahara from the miserable camps of Tindouf. Our home was close to the Smara campsite. They could not provide us with a residence. They provided the tent itself, but it was not in its normal state. My uncle took his camels and left. My last contact with him was a couple of years ago. Is there anything more beautiful than living in the desert where you see the full moon and a sky that you do not see elsewhere? The beautiful, vast, and gorgeous sky lets you see stars with unmatched clarity— no buildings, structures, or wires conceal it. I was at a loss, by all accounts. I'm Ahmed, son of Hassan, and I have nothing now. I left my mother, whom I love so much, my dad, whom I adore, and my sister Hasania. I said to my dad two nights earlier that we should leave for the Sahara to look for my uncle Salem. He had taken his camels and headed to the core of the Sahara to get away from these thieves – as my uncle calls them "Polisario Militia."

He headed to the unknown desert because these people harassed him.

My dad said in retort: Be silent, boy, do not talk like that. These people have no mercy. They imprisoned and killed many people.

I interrupted him saying: You and I both know what I mean. If we stay here, it will not bode well for us.

I know, but we have no choice.

It is our honor, father. Don't you notice that S.H—this dog—is interested in my sister Hasania?

What can I do when he carries a gun, and he is a leader?

Let him go to hell, him and the Polisario. . We cannot stand this any longer, father.

You should give this up. I will find a solution. You are still young, take care of your studies.

We will go to Uncle Salem.

I will find a good time to go.

Even at school, they hit us with their big stick and hurt us all.

I experienced you as a man. You should be patient; patience is the key to relief from anything.

The dialogue between my dad and I ended.. I was eleven years old at the time, studying at Smara Elementary School. The teachers were tired, and some of them were relatives of the ignorant Polisario. My persistent study cost me a lot. I had no choice except to obey my dad. The image of this trifle S.H has not disappeared. He claims that he has known us for a long time, including my uncle Salem who fled to the unknown desert.

At that time they came to us, they took my dad. Yes, this S.H person entered my home and interrogated my father. He asked him about my uncle, to which my dad answered that he knew nothing. In fact, he does not know anything about my uncle's whereabouts. S.H was looking at my sister with a dirty look. No one said a word to him, then he got up and headed to the other African man who was working with them. He was from Mali, as we knew from the neighbors. He was a stranded immigrant with no money to offer to Polisario. He took money from immigrants who crossed this area and forced them to work for them.

I'll bet that no one will stay here. Either they all die or flee. My friend Bilal who studied with me during the first and second grade was captured by the Polisario. He was taken to Spain, where a Spanish family adopted him. They adopt as they want. They come here and take whomever they want to Spain, and when he quarrels with his family, they refuse to return him back. He has his own world. I saw him when he returned once with the Spanish. They came to see how the Sahrawi lived. S.H continued to visit our home, bringing milk and sardine cans. I hated seeing him. He would bring dessert for my sister Hasania who was not happy with these gifts.

When he left, my dad said: He will on Thursday and we can search for Salem in the desert.

My mom said angrily: What does this dog want? What did he say to you, Hasania?

Hasania said with fear: He wants to marry me.

My dad said angrily: Is this what we are missing? To marry a criminal, oh my God. How rude is this man? He is older than me, yet he wants to marry a very young girl.

My mom said with fear: They raped Rahim's daughter because her family needed gas.

I said sadly: I heard about that. Whenever she wanted a gas bottle, the dog who was in charge raped her.

My mom responded while looking at my dad: Shall we wait here for the fire to come?

My dad said sharply: He thinks that he can buy us off with sardine cans or a bag of milk.

Then he said to my mom: Prepare our things. We shall leave at night and pull down the tent silently.

I said with fear: What if they catch us?

My dad said with trust: We will tell them that we are changing the position of the tent. Do not tell them we are escaping from here.

The situation was tense in our home. My mom said that they were taking the kids to Cuba, and I was afraid for Ahmed. My father responded peacefully, "It is just a matter of time until we leave and turn back to Morocco after we enter the desert and take Salem with us if we find him. Allah knows his location now. These days we have lived here were not happy days. They reminded me of the past."

Once, I departed in the evening to chase locusts whose swarms were everywhere; then, I found Bilal. We were young. He said to me: They will take me.

Where?

To Spain

What is there?

My dad said that there is good food, bread, meat, and dessert.

Is there dessert?

Yes

How did you know they would take you?

They came to our home and said that they had chosen me to go there.

How did they choose you? How did they know about you and not about me?

They took my photo to the Spanish family.

God damn them. Why didn't they take me? I'm smarter than you at school.

I will leave school for you. I will be happy to leave. What is there at school except for Abdulghaffar's whip and his big stick?

I will ask my dad to send me to Spain.

How?

There is a program I have heard about.

What is it about?

They will send the children to Spain on vacation.

Thus, you will find me there, and we will roam together in Spain.

Shall your new family allow you to accompany me?

Sure, otherwise, I will leave them.

Will you?

Yes.

You cannot leave them.

Why?

I do not know. You might become a prisoner.

No, you are jealous of me.

Why should I be jealous of you? Is it because you will be a servant to the Spaniards?

I will not become a servant.

Bilal cried, but I said to him: Do not be sad. You are not a servant.

I will tell dad what you said about me.

No, do not tell him. I'm just kidding.

You want me to stay here to die starving. There is not even food available. There is just sand and insects.

You are right.

My dad said to me that Spain is better than the desert.

That is right. Spain is better than the desert.

Ask your dad to take you to Spain to find what you desire there.

I like to eat bananas.

In Spain, there are bananas, biscuits and a lot of desserts.

I will tell my dad today.

In fact, I told my dad that I wanted to go to Spain, but he was firm. He said to me that they take them to be servants of the Spaniards, and we do not want to be servants of the Spaniards or even to those who do not know what they are doing.

I said to him: Why are we poor, dad?

My dad said while looking at the desert: Poverty is not shameful. Shame is serving the colonizer and licking his feet.

Who are the colonizers?

The ones who robbed our country— these are fools. They believe that the Spaniards love them. Why did Spaniards come back here?

I do not know.

You robbed our country. Why should you come back to it and feel sorrow for its people?

I do not know.

It is a game, and nobody realizes it. These mercenaries spoil everything, even the purity and the chastity of the desert.

What is the purity of the desert, dad?

The desert is pure sand and a nation those people do not know. They know whiskey bottles, impudence, and raping girls.

Why should we stay here, dad?

One day, we will leave this misery.

In the morning, my mom woke up early and fed the sheep some bread. They had become skinny. There was no grass, and it was getting hot. She came back as if she remembered something suddenly.

She said: If S.H arrives, throw the milk on his face. We do not want it. Do not drink this milk. We need him to know that we do not want him, and he is unwelcome.

He said he would bring his daughter to us.

I said to my mom: Why is he bringing her?

I do not know. He wants her to get to know Hasania.

Hasania said angrily: I do not want to know her.

My mom said while preparing tea and while we were still in our beds: We do not want to get to know anybody. What we suffered through is enough. There is no food for the sheep.

My dad woke up upon hearing this sentence and said: I will take away the sheep today and hope that I find something

My mom said angrily: What will you find? You will find nothing except sand.

My dad said: What do you want? Shall I sell them to die of starvation?

My mom responded: I did not say you sell them.

My dad said: If I were a member of a band of thieves, then my position would be better, but I will never be with them. I will get out of this hell.

My mom said desperately: Oh, God! Where should we go? I'm afraid we might be lost in the desert.

My dad said confidently: We will not be lost since I know it inch by inch, and if we do not find Salem, we will turn around and go back to Morocco as it is a merciful nation.

I said to my dad:

They say, dad, life in Morocco is much better.

My dad responded:

Yes, people are fine in Dakhla, Laayoune, and Smara, and they live the best life, not like this prison.

I got out of the tent to watch the sunrise. Perhaps the sunshine was the most gorgeous in this area. The sunrise takes me away. Now, my sister and I are on buses with our father and mother. The scene has changed. I see it is gloomy now, and sadness is killing me when I look outside. I said to my dad: Where are they taking us, dad?

My dad said soothingly: To Tindouf village.

Why are we going there?

To travel to Cuba.

My mother was crying. My dad said to her: Ahmed is a man, Fatima. Do not worry about him. Cuba is not bad. He will study there and come back.

My mom asked: When will he come back?

My dad said: I do not know, but he will come back. His absence will not be long.

My mom said, blaming my dad: Didn't I tell you to hurry and go to the desert? You did not want to go any time but Thursday!

Don't worry. Nothing will happen to Ahmed. He will come back strong and healthy. Most importantly, he will be able to study. Ahmed is a hardworking student and will come back with a certificate.

My mom said sadly: How can a certificate be useful here?

My dad said angrily: Shut up, woman. Nothing will happen to him. Do not scare the boy.

My mom was silent, and my dad said: Take care of yourself.

I was crying when I saw my mom crying, then we got off the buses to the Tindouf military airport, and Algerian helicopters arrived to take us to the capital. Cries were loud, and the ululates were mingled with mothers' cries. Many heavy tears fell. My dad and mom returned broken-hearted to the tent and found Hasania crying. She told them that S.H came to her and sought to seduce her. He said he would bring whatever she wanted, whether it be biscuits, dessert, milk, sardines, or the clothes she needed, but she refused. Thus, he threatened that he would kill her father. My dad was furious, and my mom said: Let us leave now.

My dad replied: Ahmed has departed, and these dogs took him as a hostage. Where should we leave him?

My mom said sadly with tears: Ahmed will take care of himself, and he will not come back for a long time.

How did you know that he would come back after a long period? I saw boys who came back after a short time.

Those boys were ill, so they returned them from Cuba. I know my son. He is not sick.

Hasania interrupted him saying: S.H told me that Ahmed would not return before a year and that he was the one who sent him away. Moreover, he will also send my dad to prison.

My mom said angrily: Is what is going on real?

My dad replied: Allah is always with those who are truly patient. We shall wait to check on Ahmed, and then we will leave.

My dad was an old man who could not handle face to face confrontations, but my mom was stronger than him. She was still young. He got married late to his wife's sister after his first wife died at an early age.

My mom said angrily, directing her speech to Hasania: Did he touch you?

Hasania said: No, I escaped out of the tent, and he departed after he had left our things..

My dad said while blaming my mom: I told you: Do not leave the tent.

My mom responded angrily: Do you want me to leave Ahmed alone? Perhaps he may not return in many years. God knows what they will do with him.

My dad said with comfort: Do not worry. I heard from Aziz, the grocer, that his son studies there, and nothing happened to him.

My mom responded while blaming him: Whatever happens, is because of you. You know that they will take him.

My dad said sadly: How could I know?

Hasania said: This man said he would imprison my dad if I refused his demand.

My mom said: I will kill him and go to jail. Let him do anything.

Then she said to my dad: Listen! If we do not leave tomorrow morning, I will not stay here for a minute. This man will kill you. Do you understand?

My dad said with fear: I understand.

My mom responded: They own everything— weapons and men. It is much easier to shoot at you and bury you in the sand of the desert. You will get only your fear. Do you understand what you say?

My dad said: So, let us wait to hear news about Ahmed.

My mom said angrily: Oh man! They'll kill you, and you say let us wait. Ahmed has departed. May God bless him. It is now your turn alongside Hasania. They will take Hasania to work as a servant for him and he will have fun with her.

Hasania said angrily: I will kill him.

My mom said: This girl is young and does not understand anything. She must leave.

My dad finally said: In the morning, we will leave and head to the east to look for Salem. We will go back if we do not find him.

My mom said: If you agreed, we would have kept Ahmed rather than him going away.

My dad said angrily: Nothing will happen to him. Trust God and prepare yourself to leave this camp, as we have no more residence in it.

I took a helicopter for the first time in my life. Numerous students sat there. An Algerian officer asked the students to be silent since some were crying. There was a group of fifth-grade students from Smara Elementary School. Hmeid, our neighbor's son, said he was afraid.

I said to him: Do not worry. Trust God.

Hmeid replied: The helicopter is very loud.

The noise is deafening.

The helicopter moved, causing a loud noise. I couldn't hear Hmeid, so I whispered in his ears: It will take off with us.

I'm scared. Hmeid said, crying.

I said to him: Nothing bad will happen. Trust God. My dad said: Recite the Quran when you are on a plane.

Which Sura shall I recite?

Whatever you like.

We recited Al-Ikhlas Sura. The students started chatting with each other. Hmeid said while crying: My dad does not want me to go.

I wept when I saw him, and I said to him: Also, my dad does not want me to go to Cuba.

Hmeid said: Are we going to Cuba?

I said to him: Yes.

Is Cuba below us?

I do not think so.

Why?

They say that Cuba is far away and that we have not reached it yet.

Look. That is a desert.

I looked through the window, and it was a desert.

I said to him: It is a desert,, and Cuba is not a desert.

Really?

Yes, Cuba has green trees.

There are remote houses. We may be approaching them.

No, still, the distance is far away.

I want to go to the bathroom.

Be patient. We are on a plane.

Hmeid put his hand on his stomach and cried. I said to him: Are you feeling queasy?

Hmeid said in pain: Yes.

I was confused about what to do, but I said to him: Be patient

He put his head on the window. He was pale. He got fed up severely. He shed tears in abundance, and then he started panting. The students who came before paid attention and pointed to the Sahrawi supervisor who attended and shouted at Hmeid: What is going on over there!?

Hmeid did not answer.

I said to the supervisor: He is tired.

The supervisor said foolishly: Did anyone hit him?

The boys said: No.

He said angrily: I ask you. Has anyone hit him?

I said to him with fear: No one, but he was in pain since we boarded the plane.

The supervisor said nervously: I do not know why they bring these sick fools. What shall I do with this donkey now? Then he added: Call him, stay away from him until I bring some water.

He went and brought water, then he splashed water on Hmeid's face and said to him: Oh Boy. Oh boy.

But Hmeid did not answer.

I was worried about Hmeid while I was listening to some cries and terrified low-voiced discussions. Some students were happy, unaware of their destination.

I looked at Hmeid and said: Hmeid, Hmeid.

However, Hmeid did not respond. He started panting, so my fears increased more. I did nothing. The supervisor was furious. I started crying, and the students were uninterested. He wanted to go to the bathroom, but I forgot to tell the supervisor.

Finally, Hmeid opened his eyes and said: Where are we?

I said to him: Hmeid, we are on the plane.

He cried again and said: I want my dad.

The supervisor arrived and said: How are you?

Hmeid was crying, so the supervisor asked him: Why don't you answer? What hurt you?

Hmeid cried, and then the supervisor said: Damn your father, you are a donkey, and the one who sent you is a donkey. Since you want to stay with your father, why did you come here? Damn the father of the one who sent you because he sends kids who wet themselves when they see a plane.

Then he turned to me and said: Take care of him till we reach Algiers, the capital.

I said to him: Ok.

Then Hmeid woke up after five minutes and said to me: I peed. I wet myself.

I said to him: Shut up. Don't tell anyone.

Then he looked through the window and started crying. I said to him: Let me sit by the window.

I moved to his place, and he started crying, saying: Look well through the window.

I looked and saw houses close to the desert, and I said to him: These are houses.

He said: I did not ask you about that. Look how high we are from the land. What happens if the plane crashes? What will happen?

I said to him angrily: We will die.

He said as if he found something: I said it. We will die.

Don't worry.

Why not? I hear its sound. It is ruined and will fall.

I said sharply: Let it fall.

Where is Cuba? Is it far away from here? It's been too long.

We are not going to Cuba.

Then, where are we going?

To Algiers, the capital.

No. They told us that we were going to Cuba.

I heard the supervisor saying that we were going to Algiers, the capital.

I don't believe you. My dad told me we are going to Cuba.

Suddenly, the supervisor arrived and said: Where is the boy?

I said to him: He is over there. I pointed to Hmeid, then he said to him: Are you alright?

Hmeid responded, and he was tired due to crying: Yes.

He asked him: Are you sick?

Hmeid said: No.

Shall I bring you some water to drink?

Hmeid was silent, then the supervisor said: I asked you.

Hmeid said: Yes.

The supervisor said: There is no room for shyness here. The shy ones should go back to their family. We need you to be strong to liberate your country.

He said that and departed while Hmeid said addressing his words to me: Who is that?

I don't know. He is the supervisor here.

I did not know that he is the supervisor here.

The supervisor arrived and brought water then he suddenly stood and said to everybody: Pay attention, students. No one should leave his place. The plane will land shortly.

The plane swayed in space and was about to fall. It seems old. Suddenly it landed quickly.

Hmeid cried severely, the students cried. My heart was broken while it was landing in an area amid the sand. I heard the Algerian officer saying to the supervisor that it was an emergency landing. It seems that the engine is faulty. The supervisor responded: Where should we place these students?

The officer said: Just a minute. We will find out.

The plane moved like a scorpion on the runway. Some students fell on their colleagues, and others were wounded, such as Hmeid, who fell off his seat.

I said to him: Is your injury serious?

He said: No.

Blood was flowing on his face. His nose was broken.

We landed at an Algerian military base in the desert. Hmeid and some students were taken for treatment. While we were sitting silently and waiting in the heat of the sun, two officers came in and took us to the dormitory and asked us to be silent, and then one of them said to the supervisor: Take care of your students.

One student asked the supervisor: Where are we?

The supervisor said: It is not your business.

When it was midday, we stayed in the heat. They brought pieces of bread. One piece for each student. While we were eating small pieces of bread, one student shouted. They said a scorpion stung him, and then Hmeid arrived. They put a plaster on his nose. I asked him: Where have you been?

He answered quietly: I was with the soldiers.

He examined my nose and gave me medicine to drink. It was a cheap analgesic medication which I know from the camps.

Hmeid said: Have you eaten? I feel hungry

I said to him: A small piece of bread. Go and ask the supervisor for bread.

Hmeid dared this time and went to the supervisor who sat on the door of the deserted ward.

The supervisor said to him: What do you want, for the second time?

I want bread.

Why didn't you take bread with your colleagues?

I was at the dispensary.

He gave him bread, and Hmeid came and was pleased with it. He said: I got a piece of bread.

Time passed quickly, and darkness approached. The supervisor said: Everyone should sleep in the designated place. There is no cover here. We are in an emergency situation.

He added: There is a bathroom outside, you can use it, but it is 100 meters away. I will guide one of you to the location to guide the students to it.

There were twenty students. It was impossible to go there since the place was crowded, then the students stopped going there when the the Algerian guard arrived and said: Stop going to the bathroom in case wolves eat you.

In fact, we heard a dog barking approaching. Everyone was afraid. Hmeid stuck closely to me, and everyone in the ward was tired, sleepy, and snored loudly.

When the sun rays started creeping into the place, the guard hit the ward's door with a stick, causing a loud sound. We got up due to the booming sound and sat in our place. The supervisor who was given a sack by a soldier did the same.

The supervisor said: I have a sack of bread and a chunk of cheese, which should be enough for the whole day.

Sweat was falling on our faces. Many students rushed behind the student who was entrusted to guide students to the bathroom. The students' faces were pale. An officer came holding a stick. He said to his assistant: Take them to physical training. After a few moments, they took us to a small yard. We began running around it with our supervisor. Some students were sick, so they could not run. A foxlike officer came and started some physical exercises. It was midday, and then they took us to the dining room to eat lentils.

Hmeid said to me: This is easier for me than the plane which was about to fall.

I smiled and said to him: Because you complained so much, the plane was about to fall, and we would have died.

Hmeid said, wondering: Where are we now?

I replied quickly: We are in the desert; we didn't even reach the capital.

Shall we stay in the desert?

I don't know.

They may bring another plane instead of this ruined plane. I saw it when I went to the bathroom.

Or they may fix it. I saw two people working on it during the morning exercises.

We slept deeply in the afternoon. But one of the trainers attended in the afternoon and knocked at the wooden door frightening the students, waking them up. He said to the supervisor that they should practice in the afternoon. We ran around the camp and then came back for cleaning.

Hmeid said: What should we clean in this sand?

I said to him: There is nothing.

The supervisor said: You must go to the dining room.

We went to the big dining room to clean it. I said to Hmeid.

This is what we came for. Cleaning.

Where is Cuba?

Hmeid laughed and said: Neither Cuba nor grieve. They tell lies. It seems that we'll live here for the rest of our life.

It is a prison. I don't know how these people live amidst this sand.

They live better than us.

How?

Everything is available for them. As for us in the camps, we find nothing.

You are right. We need recommendations and connections to get a gas bottle, and a connection for milk, and another connection for sardines.

You reminded me of my dad. I don't know what happened to him now.

What will happen to them? It is the prison of camps where we only find Abdo the barber, and Mahmoud, the grocer. Other than that, there is just sand and the Polisario's vehicles.

I will say something, but promise that you won't tell anyone whatever happens.

I won't tell anyone. You are my brother who helped me on the plane.

My dad will escape.

Where would he go?

He will escape to the desert to look for my uncle Salem who was absent a while ago.

Where can he find him in this vast desert?

I don't know, but he'll escape later.

Where should he escape?

To Morocco.

They say that Morocco is better than these camps that live in deprivation. My relatives there live with dignity.

This is what I heard.

At dawn, my dad carried his items on our only camel and headed east towards the desert. My dad said to my sister Hasania and my mother: If we see the Polisario in the desert, we'll say we are looking for water for our sheep.

My mom said, consoling: May God bless us. Do you know wells nearby lest we die of thirst?

I know them. I grew up in this desert. How do I not know it?

Everyone walked away from the camp, and after half an hour, they got out of the camp area. The sun began to make its presence known. The sheep were tired. At that point, my dad decided to sit down, and he said to my mom: we will rest here for a short time.

My mom said: We have to get to the nearest well in the area.

My dad replied: It is more than ten miles away.

Why do you let us keep going?

I feel tired.

May God bless our journey.

Hasania interrupted and said: It would be better if we stayed in the camp.

My mom said angrily: We left the camp. Isn't it for the sake of your eyes, and in order not to leave you as prey to S.H and then not to let the sin occur?

My dad replied: Shut up Fatima. This speech is useless now.

My mom said angrily: Didn't you hear what she said?

My dad said: Oh, Fatima, we are in trouble. and you are looking at trivial things.

Hasania cried and said: I will not go with you.

My dad said: Hasania, my darling, we do not need more foolishness. Do you think that the desert trip shall be a vacation? We will lose much in it.

My mom said: I'm worried about the sheep from the sand. We don't know where to go.

My dad said: We will go to the nearest well to rest. He said that and drank a little water that he carries in the water bottle and gave it to Hasania to drink.

My mom said: I'm getting old.

My dad's eyes were teary and said: I didn't sleep yesterday. I saw Ahmed in a dream. I was asking him to eat with us, but he refused.

My mom said: It might be good.

Hasania said: What does this dream mean, dad?

My dad said: I don't know my daughter.

They built a small tent to protect them from the sun, and sat under it, then my mom said: I've got an idea.

My dad said quickly: What is it?

My mom replied: Since you know the location of the well, what do you think about you and Hasania leading the sheep to the well since it is nearby, and I'll stay with our things?

Hasania asked: Will you be able to find your way back, dad?

My dad said confidently: Yes, I know the area.

My mom said: Then, trust in God.

We slowly started to be familiar with this lonely, awful place. Sands were surrounding the camp from all sides. We had to get up in the morning, run around the camp, return to the kitchen, have a piece of bread and a small piece of cheese, an olive and then sit on the ground in the ward. The smell of the boys' sweat was filling the space. No one could change their clothes even though we were here for three days. Nobody asks anymore when we go to Algiers, the capital. Even some students believed that we are in Cuba now.

When it was about seven o'clock, our supervisor Hassan arrived and said that we all must stand in the yard without exception and be in rows to avoid laziness.. We hurried to the nearby yard and stood in front of Hassan. He stood about ten minutes like a statue till students were bored of standing. Finally, an Algerian officer came. He talked to him and departed. We started doing physical exercises till the sun rose, and it was very hot, then we got into the ward. Every student started chatting with his neighbor. Hmeid was with me, and he would never leave me.

Hmeid said: Shall we stay here?

I said to him: I don't know.

I feel hungry.

Me, too.

I have backache.

Because we sleep on the floor.

I have a headache.

Me too.

Shall we stay here?

God knows.

It is hot. We almost suffocate in this ward.

That's right.

One can not stretch his legs.

There is neither might nor power, strength except with God. This plane has not known ruins except when we boarded it.

I saw it standing.

It seems it has malfunctioned and will not leave.

Don't they have other planes?

If they had planes, they would have brought them.

Is it reasonable?

They may be on the way to fixing it.

When will they come?

I don't know.

What happens if they can't fix it?

We will stay here.

Shall we stay here for the rest of our life?

I said, laughing: Yes, maybe. I don't know.

If we ask them to leave us and go to our families across the desert.

Do you know the way?

No.

So, how could we return?

We will keep going till we arrive.

Where should we arrive?

To our homes.

Oh. Where is your home?

At Smara Camp.

God knows where our homes are now.

Do you live in a tent?

And I don't know where the tent is now.

What do you mean?

My dad might have left the camp.

Where should he go?

To the desert.

What is there in the desert?

Everything.

There are sardines, milk, and bread in the camp.

The desert has got everything. You won't find anyone from the Polisario that hurts your life and hits you.

Food is scarce here.

We are guests here. They didn't know the plane would fall.

What is the solution?

There is no solution.

Where is the Polisario?

They are in the camps celebrating.

What are they celebrating?

They are celebrating their fake victories.

Do you hate them?

Yes.

Why?

Because they are bastards, including the teachers and the camp's manager, and the guards that control people's life.

That's right.

What is the difference between this isolated camp in the desert and the camps we live in?

Nothing.

Dogs come at night, and hyenas attack people.

And here, also.

There is less food here.

Here, it is the same.

People die due to their aches.

The same is here.

Do you know that Cuba might be better?

Yes.

There, there is sea and trees.

Here there is sand.

There are streets there.

Here we have sand.

There are homes there.

Here we have a tinned sheet.

There is food over there.

Here we have hunger.

Hmeid was just about to finish his sentence whenHassan, the supervisor, said: "Be prepared for lunch." We walked in a line one behind another and stood in front of the kitchen's window.

The cook was inside the kitchen and gave each group a big tray of rice with little meat on it. In the blink of an eye, everything disappeared. The hungry leapt on it.

A student said: Bring another tray. We have not eaten yet.

One student went with a tray, but the cook expelled him and took the tray.

Hassan, the supervisor, said: "Go back to the ward."

"Lunch was over," he said and then went to the cook to devour more food while we were hungry. The morsels we had eaten were clearly not enough.

One of the students said while we were going back: We will starve here.

Another one said: We want to go home.

One of them said from the left side: Shut up in case supervisor Hassan hears you and then hits you.

The student responded angrily: Let him hit me. We are not slaves here.

We arrived at the ward, sat on the floor that we headed to because it is somewhat cool.

Hmeid said: It seems that we'll die here. Food is insufficient.

I said angrily: Let them leave us in the desert to be eaten by beasts. It is better than staying in this place.

Hardly five days passed. They were very difficult days. Our bodies and our souls were tired, and our hearts stunned the throats. Until we heard the sound of a helicopter, then Hmeid cried loudly. Supervisor Hassan said: You, boy, shut up.

The new helicopter landed on the designated area. One of them came and told supervisor Hassan to be ready. After about an hour, an Algerian officer asked us to board the helicopter beside supervisor Hassan. At that point Hmeid started shouting, then supervisor Hassan hit him, and took him to the helicopter.

He said to me: You are responsible for him.

Hmeid didn't calm down from crying. I gave him water, then the supervisor arrived and said: In a few hours, you'll arrive in Algiers. There is nothing to worry about there. Please be calm. Hmeid was silent because of fear. The helicopter started to fluctuate in the sky heading for Algiers. Hmeid was saying: It will fall down once again.

Don't worry. It won't fall. We'll arrive in Algiers and there we'll relax and won't feel anything. Please, stop this nonsense, Hmeid.

Hmeid was silent. I started peeping through the window. The Desert is horrible. How do we live in this fearful space and love it?

Glory be to Allah.

Finally, Hmeid slept, and I praised God for that. I spoke to another student on the opposite side.

The student said: Are we going to pursue studies in Cuba?

I said to him: I don't know

How can we learn the language?

I do not know.

There were many questions, and no one knew the answers.

My dad was exhausted and fell due to a sunstroke while looking for Salem, his brother in the desert. My mom carried him on the camel's back and continued walking. At dawn, my father's promise was right.

My uncle, Salem, was building his house in a remote area near a well in the heart of the desert.. He welcomed my mom warmly and helped my dad get down from the camel after they washed his face.

My mom said: God saved us; we were about to die. If you were farther, we would not reach you, but Hassan knew the unknowns of the desert and was able to get us this far. Unfortunately, he had sunstroke at the latest moment.

Uncle Salem said: Welcome.

My dad told him about everything and said: Now they may be looking for us in the camp.

My uncle Salem said: Relax, no one is going to look for you.

My dad said: Really?

My uncle, Salem said: They don't care about anyone.

My mother said: They'll search for us, in particular, and will get mad.

My uncle said, wondering: Why?

My mom said: There is a story we will tell you about.

My uncle got up and slaughtered a sheep. The family relaxed inside his home, and the night had fallen.

My mom whispered to my dad: They won't leave us.

Yes.

S.H will come to look for Husniyya. He'll be mad.

We will kill him here.

No, it would be better if we tell your brother and leave this area.

They'll never reach here.

They have vehicles. They'll come. Nothing will hinder them.

We will tell him in the morning and see what happens.

Is Dakhla city in Morocco far away?

Yes.

How would we escape?

We'll find a solution.

Everyone heard the sound of a ferocious dog in the neighborhood. My uncle owned a group of vicious dogs that swept the area at night.

My uncle Salem got up and lit the lamp he was holding. He directed it against the dogs which were chasing an animal. My dad got up with my uncle. My uncle said: Go back to sleep. You are tired.

Don't worry. What is there?

My uncle said: I think it is the spotted hyena I saw three days ago in a den ten kilometers away.

Are there hyenas in the area?

Yes, but the dogs are strong. I was about to catch this hyena last time.

They are hungry, and they can't leave the sheep. They need to steal something.

The dogs were panting. My uncle lit the lamp against them. They were tired. It seems that they were involved in a fierce battle.

My dad said: Three dogs followed by a hyena.

My uncle replied: It is a fierce hyena. It thinks it is the master of the area, and no one can stop it.

What should we do?

These dogs are not easy. They will tear it if they catch him, but the problem would be the other hyenas with it.

Does he have anything?

Yes, if they came together, they would make a problem for us. Last winter, they attacked us fiercely. If it weren't for my gun, many sheep would have been killed.

May God bless and help you.

Come, let's drink some coffee.

My uncle put the coffee pot on faint and dim embers, and then they started drinking coffee in front of the house.

My dad said: We should leave the area and return to Morocco.

What is the benefit of that?

The situation in Morocco is better. Our brothers in Dakhla and Laayoune find all the care.

Still, it is early. Can we take our sheep there?

Yes, the area is wide and is enough for all here. If we die, nobody will know about us.

Trust in God.

One of the dogs barked, and then my uncle got up and said: Another hyena may have returned.

We arrived at Houari Boumediene Airport. It was the first time we landed in an airport. No one was there. It was a lonely place except for some soldiers who were going back and forth. One of them came and read the names of the students. The supervisor took the passports that Algeria issued to us. He went down. We kept looking eagerly at the dessert and the food in the middle of the hall. Hmeid said while contemplating the restaurant that sold sorts of cakes.

Look! They have delicious food.

I said to him: You'll eat more delicious food in Cuba.

I don't think it is luxurious.

Have you been to Cuba to judge?

While we were waiting, supervisor Hassan arrived and called the students. We marched in a corridor and headed to the helicopter where a soldier was standing.

He was inspecting the students, and then we boarded the plane through a long passage. We sat on seats, and the sound of the engine roared. This time, the situation seemed better than the helicopter. However, Hmeid started panting. I said to myself: May God make us reach Cuba safely.

The plane started moving, and the captain announced instructions we couldn't understand.

Some students were silent and terrified, while others started to sleep. Supervisor Hassan had advised us while walking between seats: Whoever could sleep. Let him sleep. When the plane reached its cruising altitude, I began to fall asleep. Hmeid

did the same. I slept many hours and woke up looking around with fear. My dad's apparition passed by when he was looking for his fleeing brother from the injustice of Polisario. I was not happy with this sleep. Moments later, Hmeid woke up. He was also scared. He couldn't hide his annoyance.

He said to me: I'm longing for my mom. I said to him that I didn't know what had happened to my family. Are they looking for Uncle Salem in the desert or not?

Hmeid peeped through the window of the plane and asked: Where are we? There is nothing but emptiness. I told him I myself don't see anything either.

Hmeid said: What is that thing walking beside the plane?

I said to him: I don't know. Something that goes with the plane might be part of it.

May God forgive dad. I said to him that I don't want to go to Cuba.

Could he have refused? The Polisario do what they want.

There was a chance to escape from the camps where we did nothing. Our neighbor fled to Morocco.

I asked my dad to escape to Morocco. There is not even food in camps.

Hmeid said in pain: I want to go to the bathroom.

I said to him: Follow these students who go to the back of the plane.

He said in fear: I'm scared. Come with me.

I went with him to the back of the plane where the bathroom is. After seconds, he began knocking at the door while crying. The flight attendant calmed him down and gave him candy.

The flight attendant said to his colleague: I don't know why they send these young boys to Cuba.

The other person said: To come back as fighters with the Polisario and liberate the Sahara.

Are these people going to establish a state? Which state in the Sahara?

The second person said: Shut up, man. Do you want to send us to jail?

We came back, Hmeid and me, to our seats in the middle of the plane, and then Hmeid said: If the plane fell, where would we be?

I said to him, laughing: We would be a thing of the past.

He responded sympathetically: No. Right. Where should we end?

The front of the plane will dig into the ground, and we'll be in the middle, but we'll die. The middle site is useless.

Hmeid said with fear: What about going back to the back of the plane?

No.

Why?

They will be angry with us-Supervisor Hassan, and the officials on the plane.

As we were talking, the in-flight announcer said: Ladies and gentlemen, fasten your seatbelts. The plane will start descending gradually and will be landing in Camaguey city (Which Cuban authorities had designated for the reception of the Saharawi students).

Hmeid said: We have arrived

Yes. We have arrived.

The plane will land.

Finally, we arrived.

Where is the city?

I don't see it.

It is still far away.

He said: We are landing in the city.

I don't see a city.

Be patient. The city will appear.

The pilot may have been lost.

Do planes get lost? That's not possible.

We don't see a city.

After a few minutes, the city will appear. Don't you notice that the plane's speed is lower?

Yes.

We'll land- He said so. There is no land here. It is all sky.

Hmeid wanted to cry. I said to him: Shut up.

The descent of the plane took a long time. Hmeid said: The pilot may have changed his opinion.

I said quickly: Maybe, he has gone to another city.

What's going on?

Nothing.

Hmeid replied angrily: Is the man fooling with us?

I don't know. The plane might have malfunctioned, such as the one we had in the Algerian desert.

We have bad luck.

I said to Hmeid: The best thing we can do is go to bed.

We closed our eyes to forget what was happening.

Fifteen minutes later Hmeid woke me up and said: We have not landed

I said to him: Forget it.

How can I forget?

You fooled me. Stop talking for a while, Hmeid. We want to know what's going on in these moments. The call was repeated, and the plane started landing. Hmeid said: We are landing.

My heart trembled in fear. Hmeid held my hand. I said to him: It seems we are landing.

In fact, the plane started landing in Camaguey. We walked through the airport. We were dazzled by the lights. We arrived at night and found Cuban soldiers. They took everything: our passports,, documents, and personal belongings.

We got into military vehicles, and we were taken to a paramilitary camp. They sent us to the ward. We sat in a hall, and supervisor Hassan asked us to be silent. Others came. They had Sahrawi faces and it seems that they work with the Cuban.

A Cuban officer came and said: You are welcome here. You are among your family; you will find whatever pleases you and then come back as soldiers to serve your country, the Sahrawi Arab Republic for the prosperity ofglobal socialism and free nations. Cuba shall be the mother of lovers of their nations and mother of the poor in the world. You should be committed to your studies and work for the future of your Sahrawi nation.

There is no room for laziness. We have Cuban laws that we should be committed to. You are still at the beginning of your life. I wish you success. Long live Cuba.

Then the Sahrawi translator asked the students to chant in Cuban language, "Long live Cuba."

The Cuban officer left, and the Sahrawi senior supervisor continued his speech, saying, "Your nation needs you, you have to care for your studies to return to your families who live on pins and needles. I know you are tired from the long trip. Now you'll have dinner then you go to bed. Tomorrow you'll wake up early for training in order to be able to struggle for the sake of your country and nation."

One of the supervisors said: "My name is Khalil," and he took us to the kitchen this time. Food was a little different. This time, we felt a bit overwhelmed then went to our beds in the ward. There might be some similarities with the Algerian camp in the desert, but this ward was better and more beautiful. As soon as we stretched ourselves in bed, one of them came and lit the lamp and asked us to sit. We sat on seats, and it seemed that a supervisor came late, and he was informed about our arrival. He looked like he was drunk.

He said suddenly: I don't want to bother you, and then we went to bed. The covers and sheets smelt like pesticides.

Hmeid said: The smell of the cover is deadly.

I told him: Don't put it on your face.

Hmeid said: How much I miss my dad.

I replied: Me, too. I don't know what happened to my family and if they had escaped or not?

Only God knows.

I miss them too much.

What should I do in the morning?

I don't know.

We talked for a long time despite being exhausted. The morning came, and one of the supervisors woke everyone up. We ran to the yard. Our day started with running along the jogging track till we got tired, then we went back to have breakfast.

Hmeid said: Do we study or train?

I don't know, we came to study, and it seems we came here to train to fight.

The new supervisor looked at us disgusted. He was fiercer than the previous one, who had disappeared. He had harsh features, his eyes were sunken with a long nose, and he was short. He spoke quickly and we could hardly understand anything. He doesn't forget to add a few Spanish words to his speech to let you know that he had spent a long time here in Cuba.

S.H was shocked when he came to the camp and found nobody. He couldn't believe himself. Where had these people gone? He was carrying gifts and sweets. He wants to be with the brunette girl whom he loves, but he didn't find Husniyya. He asked the neighbors, and they told him that they woke up and didn't find anyone. They have fled like what his brother – Salem did previously.

He said to himself: They haven't gone far. He took with him his companion- young Omar- who came from Mali. Everyone carried a machine gun and got into a four-wheel drive vehicle. Their driver was with them. He won't lose Husniyya easily and will make her father pay the price.

He believed that things were moving in the right direction, and that they'd agree that she'll work with him in the corporation he ran in lieu of getting sardine, milk and bread but this didn't happen. S.H said to Omar - his companion: Where do you expect we will find them?

Omar naively said: We might find them on the borders with Morocco.

S.H said: You are clever, Omar. They are heading now to Morocco's borders.

It won't be long, and we'll find them. The car took them to Morocco's borders. S.H said: The borders with Morocco are long.

Omar responded: We'll walk parallel to Smara camp, and then look for the rest of the wall. They found some mercenaries near the Polisario's borders and asked them but there was no answer, then they continued walking north parallel to the wall. S.H said to the driver: Calm down. There are people walking near the wall.

The car stopped near a group of people. They were only a group of Polisario militia coming back from a mission. S.H was frustrated and said to Omar: We didn't find anyone here.

Omar said: The area is not big, we'll find them.

Night fell, and we didn't find any traces. We'll get up tomorrow morning and continue searching.

Omar replied: Why don't we tell more soldiers to help us in searching?

S.H said: There is no need for that. It will be enough if we chase them; we might find this man and put him in jail for his actions.

This is what it should be.

S.H came home tired and found his son who said to him: Why don't you let me go with the students to Cuba?

He said to his son: This is not your time. Get out of my face because demons roar in front of me.

Amena, his daughter, came and said: Have you brought food, dad?

He replied quickly: No, I didn't need to. I had eaten outside.

S.H, whose wife died of cancer, had started to let loose and chase girls and married women alike. But he was much too fond of Husniyya. He was preoccupied. He couldn't sleep. Is it believable that Husniyya fled? Her face looked like the moon and eyes were wide, and her tan was lovely and smooth.

What should he do? He communicated with his companion, Omar. He said to him: Beware of being late in the morning.

I'll come early.

But where should we search?

We'll search in the opposite direction near the Algerian borders and these areas.

It is a very wide land.

There were sheep with them, so they'll not escape for a far distance.

Yes, you are right.

Goodbye.

He turned off the telephone, rested a little, then he called his son, Mahmoud, and said to him: Don't worry. I'll not send you to Cuba, I'll send you to Spain.

My friends went to Cuba.

There are flights to Spain. You'll spend the summer in Spain. It's better than Cuba.

I want Cuba.

You'll not go to Cuba. Spain is better. You'll find what pleases you, and then you will pursue your studies.

Chapter 2.

My dad told my uncle everything. The two quickly decided to leave for the Mauritanian border area because it was the nearest. They entered Mauritania, and there near one of the desert wells they stopped in order to head for one of the Mauritanian oases.

My dad said: Shall S.H arrive here?

My uncle replied: He might arrive, but I don't think so. He can't enter here.

What prevents him? I think he believes that you'll go to Morocco's borders to enter Morocco.

I don't know.

Kareem and Husniyya got water from the well and watered camels and sheep.

My dad said: Hurry up; we don't want this man to follow us here. We are still close to the Algerian borders. We want to get inside Mauritania.

They rested near a nearby stone, waiting for the pots to be filled with water.

My uncle, Salem said: We need water. Animals are too thirsty.

My mom called Husniyya saying: Let Kareem get water, come and help me.

My mom opened a cloth bag she was carrying on the back of a camel. She was sweating.

She started making date porridge under the shade of a rock. Husniyya helped her by bringing flour, water, and fat, while my uncle, Salem, was asking mom to hurry up because Kareem was about to finish his mission.

My mom was calming him, saying: We are far away and entered Mauritania.

My uncle replied: We don't know. He might come behind us.

My mom finished cooking the porridge and they began eating quickly.

Kareem said: I need soup (Tabikha).

My uncle Salem said: Upon arrival, Salma will make that because she is skillful in her job.

My mom replied quickly: Where would we bring meat from?

My dad said: We want to sell sheep.

My uncle added: And I want to sell sheep, too. I have got nothing more. We need to buy tea and sugar.

My dad said: Camps destroyed us; we no longer take care of our sheep.

Everyone finished eating, and then hurried between sand dunes.

My uncle Salem said: I remember coming with my dad to a mountain near here.

My dad said: The mountain will be on the left. I know it well. I often reach it.

The small caravan moved towards the oasis. It was not close. Sheep were thirsty after a long march. Kareem was the caravan leader, and my uncle asked him not to hurry, while my dad asked him to stop after each kilometer because he had heartache.

At each rest, my dad says: May God not help them. They took my son to Cuba.

My uncle said: They wanted to take Salma to Cuba. If I had not escaped, Salma would have been in Cuba now.

My mom said: What are they doing in Cuba?

My uncle laughed and said: What would they do but shamelessness?

The caravan then moved quickly and silently.

We ran at five o'clock in the morning around a camp. It was dark, we couldn't see around, then we went to the restaurant and had breakfast. I was heartbroken and my sense of loss was great. Where is my dad, mom and Hasania now? We got a piece of cheese, a piece of bread and a cup of tea then we went back to the ward. We prepared ourselves to get out to the yard for physical training exercises that lasted for an hour, and then we sat with the Cuban trainer. He started training us on machine guns – how to assemble and disassemble them. However, we took a rest at ten o'clock. We were surrounded by trees. The atmosphere was different from that of the camp. Summer was hot and trees were surrounding the camp. The wind was blowing from the sea direction. We understood that Cuba was an island, and that we live there now on the youth island where many students from different countries study. Now Cuba has become our father and mother as the Cuban officer who has given a lecture said about love of the country. After eleven o'clock we had a lecture by the supervisor Alsaleh who said that the Moroccan enemy was stalking us.

And we must be cautious, train on weapons in order to restore our land from the Moroccan enemy. I remembered that a year before one of our relatives came disguised and said: Morocco is one million times better than this hell that you live in, and that he'll smuggle us from the camps, but my dad refused despite my mother's approval.

I got bored of this utterance" The occupying Moroccan enemy", and that these mercenaries are the fighters, but I kept silent as my dad told me.

I loved the pine trees; we didn't have pine trees in camps. Pine had a distinguished smell my nose started to be familiar with. Each one got a box to put his items and bed. Hmeid insisted on having his bed close to me so we might talk at night.

The officer told us that we have training in the afternoon on grenade throwing. I said to myself: Did we come here to study or fight? In fact, after having lunch, which I didn't like, they took us to a field. There was an earthen berm, and the officer started throwing a model grenade. He pulled the lightning and threw it, then he threw a real one and it made a horrible sound. Hmeid said to me afterwards that he wet himself.

Each one moved forward and threw a model grenade except Hmeid who trembled of fear, so the trainer excluded him.

Hmeid said to me: Is it heavy?

I said to him: No.

I was afraid it might explode in my face.

I said laughing: There is nothing. It is a simple thing, you offended us.

No, this is too much for us to deal with.

It is not much or nothing. You gave a bad impression about our lane in the camp.

No one knows that I'm from your lane.

But you are my friend.

We came back and found that the cook had prepared dinner. We arrived at dusk. We got out of vehicles near the ward, where there was a long avenue surrounded by trees.

The kitchen is located behind us. We sat in the dining ward eating dinner, which consisted of beef with potatoes. The beef leftover was recycled into another new meal. We washed the dishes and returned to the ward.

Hmeid said: I want to pray the Maghrib prayer.

Hmeid and I prayed near the bed, then everyone stretched on his bed.

Hmeid said: This life is tiresome this way.

I smiled and said to him:

The barber will come tomorrow and shave everyone's hair.

He said angrily:I don't want to shave.

You'll shave despite your well.

Do you know? I wish I could get out to see what is there beyond the trees.

There is sugar cane, palm trees and pine trees.

How did you know?

I saw from the number of vehicles we rode in.

You were at the window. I wasn't at the window so I couldn't see. Nothing was there except trees.

There are peasants.

What are they doing?

Planting.

Are there cars?

I didn't see cars.

Rather than peasants

Trees.

The caravan headed to another well closer to
Mauritania than Morocco. The surprise was that
S.H had arrived at that well which they were
camping near it, but it was the limit the two couldn't
trespass lest they were lost in the Sahara. Then S.H
said: It seems I'm losing her forever.

Omar said:

There are many more. You could find one
better than her.

I can't, Omar. I loved her. I don't want to lose
her.

You'll forget her as time passes by.

Oh, if I could arrest her father, I would tear
him and feed him to the hyenas of the desert.

Yes.

Which country do you believe he fled to,
Omar?

I don't know. He might have gone to Morocco
or Mauritania or remained in Algeria.

Will he remain in Algeria?

Yes.

The desert in Algeria is wide. He might have gone to the desert and disappeared in a nearby city.

Yes, He might be in Tindouf camps. We'll search in Tindouf and the neighborhood.

Or Biskra

Therefore, we'll search in Biskra and the neighborhood.

Why should we keep searching? Why don't we ask the neighbors once again? They have the solution.

Do you believe so?

Sure. He'll tell them about his whereabouts. We should arrest their neighbor-Ameen.

Does Ameen know their whereabouts?

Sure, he knows. They won't go before telling him where they go.

Hurry up. Let's get into the car and go to the camp. They might have returned.

They got into the car and returned to the camp and held Ameen, the old man. They took him for interrogation in a secret prison in Al Raboni.

S.H sat in a small office on a desk while Ameen – the old man- sat on a rickety chair.

S.H said: You should tell me, Uncle Ameen, where did your neighbor Haj Hassan go?

The man said frightened: I swear I don't know anything about him.

S.H said angrily: How don't you know anything about him? He told you where he was going and which lane he would follow.

He didn't tell me. He might have gone to another part of Algeria.

S.H paid attention more and said: Did he say anything to you? Algeria, Yes Algeria. You are an amazing uncle, Ameen. He is the enemy of the revolution. He must have told you which city he would go to, Biskra or Tindouf.

The man said with fear: Maybe Biskra.

Oh, Biskra.

I don't know for sure.

How don't you know? I'll make you wish death and you do not find it if you don't tell me about the enemy of the revolution and the enemy of the Sahara.

He went to Biskra, but he'll go to Tindouf first.

So, we'll find him in Tindouf now.

I don't know.

Get out of my face. Before I trample you, then he called Omar and said: He says he has gone to Tindouf now.

Omar said cheerfully. Didn't I tell you so?

Sure, you are right, Omar. Prepare the car. Let's go to Tindouf. I'll crush this man. He is the enemy of our country.

You are right.

The car headed to Tindouf. There was an Algerian guard who intercepted them, but they introduced themselves and were permitted to enter Tindouf , but they didn't find anything.

S.H said: He has deceived us.

He said to Omar quickly: I've got an idea, but I was afraid to say it.

What is it?

We take into consideration he left the Sahara if we don't find him in Bskra. He must be in a camp, and might have left Smara to Laayoune camp, for example or to Ausserd camp.

You are right. How did this idea not cross my mind? In fact, we'll look for him in the camps. We might find him. He might not have left the area.

Yes.

Husniyya asked my dad about the place they arrived to, and he said to her: It is Azoki

They built their tents near an oasis in Azoki. It was hot, and the sheep were in severe dengue. My uncle Salem said: It would be better if we sell the sheep lest they die.

My dad said angrily: What are you saying, Salem?

As you heard.

The sheep are the source of our livelihood.

The situation is difficult; there is not much water in this area.

Uncle Salem said: We have no choice but to leave quickly.

My dad, the elder one said: But we'll stay for a month. We are tired. We'll try to manage ourselves with the water.

They started to buy water at a high price; nevertheless, they stayed in the area.

When my mom sat with Hasania, Hasania said: I waisted my studies.

My mom replied: You'll compensate for it in Morocco.

When will we arrive in Morocco?

I don't know.

Some went to Cuba.

Will you go to Cuba? What will you do there? I'm worried about Ahmed. What about you? Sure, you'll be lost.

Some others went to Algeria.

What will you do in Algeria?

I will study.

Get up and make tea, as if all this suffering is not for your sake!

My Uncle Sam and dad got into the tent. My uncle said: Is there any news about the camp?

There is no news.

This area is isolated. We know nothing about it. I've got an idea....

What is it?

My uncle said: To come back undercover (disguised).

My dad laughed a lot at the idea and said: What do you benefit from that?

To see that bastard.

The important thing is that we have left him.

No, we'll not leave him.

No, I'll not leave him.

We are done with this issue, Salem.

How are we done? We've lost a lot of sheep and camels? He is fighting us in everything. I'll not leave him whatever the cost.

Salem!

I don't have any money left. We paid money to drink water. What shall we do if we stay longer?

We will not stay here for a long period.

We will not stay for a long period.

Husniyya distributed tea. My mom said: We should hurry in going to Morocco.

My dad replied: However, we should be cautious. If we are captured, it would be a catastrophe.

This is right.

My mom said: We walked all this distance to fall in their hands. Indeed, it would be a catastrophe.

Kareem, who just came, said: Living here is unbearable.

My dad replied: Is living in the camp better? It's a life that shortens life.

Uncle Salem said: We need to solve this problem; otherwise, we will be beggars in this area.

My dad said quietly: Let's wait for two other weeks, relief may come.

Husniyya replied: The keeper of the orchard said we have to leave this place.

Uncle Salem said: He is an idiot. He has nothing. I talked with the owner of the orchard, and he didn't object. I told him that we are guests and would leave.

My dad said: There is no power but from God. God shall not forget us.

Salma, my cousin, said: This area is another world. I began to feel that we live in a strange world.

Husniyya said laughing: The jinn shakes the palm trees at night.

My dad said reprimanding: Shut up, girl.

My uncle responded: Why would she stop? She went yesterday with the moon's light and imagined that one of them was over a palm tree.

Kareem said: What did he do above the palm tree?

My uncle replied: I don't know, but I'm scared.

My Dad said: There is no need to go at night. We are guests here.

My uncle replied: I got outside into the open area.

My mom replied: I didn't like this man who guards the palms. I felt that he was a devil.

My uncle said: Do you mean the man who was above the palm at night?

My mom replied: I don't know.

Chapter 3.

Supervisor Alsaleh came at night, and said to us we should study hard, and that we shall move to an intermediate school among sugar cane farms. In fact, we moved the next day to a new school among fields. Sugar cane farms were stretching to wide distances as well as other lemon and citrus trees, tomato, and cauliflower.

We went once again to a new ward- Hmeid and I. The smell of trees surrounded us from all directions. The school was not far from the fields. We started learning Spanish, and the teachers were Sahrawi teachers and Cubans.

The first day, a tall teacher with black eyes, coarse hair and a long nose entered. His name was Rashid. He said he was like us, and we shouldn't worry. This is our destiny, and we only came here for our country. He added he would teach us Arabic and social studies.

At first sight, I remembered the camp and how we lived there. Three months passed, and they were a mixture of misery, unhappiness, and sadness, then we moved to a new school. Time passed quickly.

We left on foot to a nearby sugar cane. The smell of sugar cane scattered in the air. Hmeid stretched his hand and took a stick from the ground.

Supervisor Alsaleh said: You are guests here. You should provide a bright image of your country.

When Hmeid heard that, he threw the stick he was holding and said to the supervisor: Beware of insects.

We arrived at the field, and my job was with a group that consisted of five individuals. We cut the weeds that grow in the big field. The Cuban farmers showed us. We walked slowly in the field and Hmeid was beside me as usual. Hmeid said: Why should we be concerned in this business?

I said to him: They deal with us as soldiers.

Do soldiers work in the fields?

Yes.

He was surprised and said: This is the first time I learned that soldiers work in the fields.

A wasp attacked us; we put our hands on our heads. Hmeid said: How long should we stay here?

A student answered: We go back for lunch then we come here.

Hmeid was astonished and said: Who told you that?

The young man responded: Alsaleh told me.

I said to the young man: How long shall we stay here?

The student said: We'll stay till dusk.

Hmeid said, astonished: Really?

The young man said: Yes.

I said quickly: I thought that we would have some time here at school.

Hmeid said: There will be time there.

A student said: What are they doing with this cane?

I said to him: They make sugar.

The young man replied: Do they make sugar from this cane?

Hmeid said: Where have they taken that group of patients yesterday?

The young man who knew details said: They took them back to camps.

I said: They won't stay here.

The young man replied: Yes, what will they benefit from?

They couldn't work on farms.

Hmeid said: Why don't they work on farms?

The young man said: They need workers.

At dusk, we were exhausted. We arrived at the accommodation in dire straits.

Chapter 4.

The sun rose, announcing a new day. Despite his grief, my dad looked east and tried to smile. While he was immersed in his contemplations, a masked man came to the tent. He welcomed him. They sat together, and the man said: I came to you from Laayoune Camp.

Welcome. What's up with you?

News are good, but your son, Ahmed, arrived from Cuba and he's sitting next to the neighbors. He asks about you and doesn't know what to do.

My dad, while pouring tea for the man, said: What's your name? God bless you.

My name is Alati.

Alati, would you do me a favor?

What is it?

Bring him here, and I will give you two heads of sheep.

I can't.

Why?

You must come and bring him to me because I came here with difficulty. I don't know the lanes, and I fear we'll perish-the two of us.

Can you handle it?

Sorry.

Wait a minute.

While they were talking, my uncle Salem arrived and looked at the man's face. And said: Are you Musa?

Who is Musa?

You are Musa, the guard in Alraboni.

No, you are wrong.

How come, man? What brought you here?

The man was silent, and my dad said: Alati, you should have lunch with us.

The man said: I'm in a hurry, please.

The man got up and rode his camel and went too fast.

My dad said, astonished: Where do you know him from, Salem?

I know him from when they arrested me in Alraboni.

What's his job?

He works as a jailer. If only he was in your house I would spit on his face. How did he come here?

I don't know.

My uncle said suspiciously: We should leave the area.

Where?

To Itar.

No.

Itar is a city, and will be exposed there.

Where should we go, then?

To Adrar.

Why don't we go to Morocco?

We'll be captured.

I suggest that we go into the main road.

How could we walk this road with our sheep and camels?

This is the best solution.

No.

Let's think about it and rest two days here. They'll not return now.

My mom arrived; I sat and drank tea with them. She said: What is there?

My dad said: We are being monitored.

My mom said: He is the guard who ascends the palm trees and monitors.

My uncle replied: Really?

My mom said: Yes, his behavior is suspicious.

While they were talking, the owner of the orchard-Omar- arrived. He said to my dad that he wanted him this afternoon to talk about a private matter, and then he went to the orchard.

My uncle said: What does this one need?

My dad replied: I don't know.

My mom said: It seems that we are in a bad area. I hear sounds every day that come from the palm top.

My dad replied: These devils rest at night after being tired during the day.

My uncle replied: I think we should leave this area.

My mom said: Really, Ahmed has returned to the camp from Cuba?

My uncle said: It is a trick by S.H to catch my brother in order to force him to bring Hasania. He is a mad person who couldn't hide his ill intentions.

My mom said: I miss you, my son.

My dad replied: Your son is in Cuba. This man is lying.

My mom said: May God keep him away from this man's wickedness.

My dad said: We should go to Morocco. It is the best solution. We won't stay here forever.

My uncle said: Morocco has improved, it has become a paradise in the region.

My mom said: It is the best solution.

My dad said: We should sell the sheep.

No, it is our livelihood.

My dad replied: We would sell them and buy whatever we want in Morocco. This is the right thing to do.

My mom interrupted, saying: That's right. It is for the best.

They all agreed to sell the sheep and go to Morocco.

Chapter 5.

Mosa went to Alraboni and met S.H. He told him about what had happened to him. S.H got angry and told him he was not clever enough. All I need and want is to marry their daughter.

He then dismissed Mosa and called Omar. He said to him: We should think about returning them to the camp before they go to Morocco.

They will stay longer in Mauritania. Omar replied positively and said that he would think of a plan to send them to the camp and put them in jail.

Omar said: Sir, this lady, Um Huda, who wants gas and milk. I will bring her to you. She cursed Polisario.

S.H said: Is she beautiful?

Omar said: Yes.

The woman entered the room. S.H was behind the office. He said to her: Welcome.

Assalam Alaikum (Peace be upon you).

S.H replied sarcastically. Peace be upon you. What is your story?

The woman said with fear: Nothing.

S.H said: How do you say nothing, you cursed the Polisario?

Why, shouldn't I curse them?

Do you need anything? Say it frankly, no one will hurt you.

We have got nothing.

Really? He said maliciously.

Yes, my husband died of diabetes, and no one cared about him.

Why didn't anyone care about him? The revolution spares no effort to guarantee health to everyone.

He got gangrene in his body, and nobody cared about him. He suffered a lot before he passed away.

We are all sacrifices for the country.

Which country?

Our country is the Sahrawi Arab Republic, which we fight for its sake, and lose our lives for in order to raise the flag.

Which country do we die for free?

Did you study?

No.

Learning is our first enemy which spoils people, then, you are against the revolution. Without learning you thought that the educated are the bastards who spoil everything.

I'm not an enemy of anyone but we'll starve to death.

How many sons do you have?

I've got three girls.

How do you earn a living?

Good people give charity.

No, no I don't believe it.

How don't you believe this? Have you gone to the camps that have got nothing except hunger? Which republic are you talking about? We don't find bread.

The republic is more important than you and the bread.

Do you feel hungry? I wonder.

Yes, we are all the redemption of the revolution.

She looked at him. He was well-built, and doesn't seem there is a sign of hunger, and said: I don't think so.

He said angrily: Do we lie?

Nobody said that you are lying, but we have got only sands to eat. When would the assistance come?

What is wrong with the assistance?

Nothing.

Say whatever you like. You won't be accountable for it, but I want to hear everything from you. I want to know the truth.

Which truth? Is there a truth?

Yes, what about the assistance?

Assistance is being stolen.

Who steals them? I don't know. You know more than me.

I asked you to say the truth, and I'll not get angry. I want to know everything.

You steal the assistance.

We. Who are we?

You. I don't know.

You mean the government.

Yes.

No. We don't steal. This is a huge accusation. Assistance goes to the poor and to everyone. You know we don't have resources.

I know. Nothing except sand.

Why did you come to the camp since you don't like the situation?

I didn't come. I found myself in it. I was born in it and lived a miserable life.

We work hard to make life better, but we face many difficulties.

Nothing changes except for the worse.

Do you know that I like your logic?

The woman was silent.

S.H says loudly: Omar, bring tea.

Omar brings tea to S.H, then he says to him: Bring another cup. He then said to the woman: You'll drink tea with me.

The woman replied suspiciously: No, thanks.

No, you'll drink. We are family. We know that everyone goes through difficult circumstances.

The woman cries. S.H says: Never mind, um Huda. You should be strong. We all go through situations. I will help you with whatever you need. I won't let you need anything such as sugar, milk, bread, sardine, and gas.

He then gave an in-depth look at her.

Hmeid became a philosopher. He said to me: We serve Cuban cigars.

We had to move in the tobacco field from the tobacco that is used for casing, and the tobacco that is used for cigar filling. We work today in the filling field. Hmeid said: There is a beautiful girl who helps in collecting the harvest.

I asked him: Did she look at you?

No.

Hmeid was brown, and it was unlikely to be loved by this blond girl.

I said to him: Talk to her using what you know in Spanish.

You are smarter than me.

I'll not talk to her. The supervisor is nearby.

Then, shut up and focus on your job.

The tobacco leaves were wide. Hmeid held one and said: Oh my God, how big is this leaf!

They take care of it.

Where are they taking these leaves?

For drying and then to factories.

They say there are girls who work in the factories.

That's right.

I got bored of school and the field. Life is tiring and boring. How long should we stay here?

Till we finish school

I want the school. It is a long walk. How would we stay here all this period? We want to get out and see people.

The boy next to me said he saw the city.

How?

He went with his relative here to that city and saw people and streets.

The sun is hot today.

We'll have another skin.

We were used to the sun.

I want to smoke.

Smoke?

Yes, I want to smoke.

Where did you get smoke from?

I will steal some from the supervisor.

What if he caught you?

What would he do? Will he hit you?

He couldn't.

Why

I'll tell the headmistress.

The headmistress will hit you as well.

No, she won't hit me.

We are here not for the purpose of smoking but for learning.

Chapter 6.

My dad changed his opinion, and he doesn't
think of selling the sheep anymore. He decided to
challenge. He said to my uncle that it would be a
cowardly step to sell the sheep and escape. If he
comes here, I'll kill him. Finally, my uncle agreed
with him. My uncle and dad decided that Husniyya
and Kareem would get engaged after a week in
order to avoid what had happened last week when
the owner of the nearby orchard came to get
engaged with Hasania. My dad told him that she
was engaged to her cousin, Kareem. Thus, their
lives passed, sands were unforgiving to anyone and
continued its attack with each gust of wind, and
Azoki continued scowling in grief.

When Omar, the owner of the orchard met my
dad in the evening, he told him he wants to leave
the orchard if the scarcity of water continues.

Omar said to my dad: Are you going back to
the Sahara?

My dad replied suspiciously while pouring tea
to Omar: God's willing.

I swear, this Sahara has no mercy. We don't know how to live. The orchard is shrinking.

The Sahara also, our life there was extremely difficult.

Omar smiled and said: I don't know how they would build a state.

As if my dad had forgotten himself, he said: Idiots, there is nothing except sand. People are dying of starvation except for some help from foreign countries.

Which country survives on aid and waits for the meeting of donors every time?

I don't know. It is a catastrophe. Refugees live like prisoners with sands and scorpions waiting for a country that does not come and shall never be able to live.

We are not in need of countries like this. A country whose people live on a little milk and sardine. It is a tragedy. How do they separate us from our country? What do these people think!

The chair glitters, even if it is in the air, it has lovers.

The other side of Morocco is better.

Sure, it's better. There are universities, projects, and beaches. What else do people want? Just a decent life.

My uncle, Salem, arrived and said: Peace be upon you.

He responded, sat, and said: Oh, how bored I'm here. I don't know, Omar, how do you live in this area?

Omar replied: God is enough. The Sahara is the Sahara, it seems it chases us. We'll leave this area because the Sahara crawls quickly to the palm.

I said to my brother, Hassan, we want to leave, but he changed his mind.

My dad interfered and said: We should wait for Satan. To stay here is better than being captured by the Polisario and tortured.

Omar said: Tomorrow I'll invite you to a feast. I got engaged two days ago.

Chapter 7.

At Alraboni, S.H visits the prisoners and interrogates some of them while they are standing, meanwhile, he keeps waking in prison. One of the prisoners found that his head was full of lice. He said to the bodyguard: Is this harmful to you?

The bodyguard said: We are outside.

Do you have a barber?

No.

They don't deserve living. How many Moroccans are here?

Thirty.

What are they doing?

They carry sacks

Aids?

Yes, and they do all the chores we need.

Why don't you use them for building?

They use them for building.

How many meals do they eat?

One meal.

It is more than enough. It was better to kill them. We don't have anything to offer them.

The prisoners' conditions were miserable. They don't even have clothes to wear except for some old clothes donated by some Spanish societies and exceeding the needs of the soldiers. The smell of sweat and insects aggravated the difficulty of life in this prison.

S.H looked at them and then got out, wishing that he hadn't caught my dad to torture him in prison. He didn't get Husniyya, yet. He called his driver, Omar and asked: Is there any news about those who fled to Azoki?

No.

Ihave been lazy lately. I want to send a group to pursue their news. They might have left this area.

This is the best solution.

When do you want to send men?

Oh, smart man, we should send one to recon the area before we send an armed group.

I'm ready.

We'll send one to imitate the seller who goes around the villages and oases carrying his goods on his camel.

It is a brilliant idea.

How long have you been working with us, Omar?

Eighteen years.

All this period and you have not absorbed what we want, man?!

Sometimes I miss things.

You should be smart. We'll go now to Um Huda. Have you brought milk and bread?

I didn't bring any.

You started to forget our date today with Um Huda despite the fact she's a beautiful woman. You might let me forget Husniyya for a short time, Omar. Hurry up and bring milk and bread from the barn.

Will the barn keeper give me?

Yes, tell him that you are on my side, and he will give you without an appointment.

I'll wait for you in the car.

It didn't take a long time, and then they hurried towards the camp.

S.H said, laughing: This is all struggle and war. It's the hearts' war. My heart starts beating towards Um Huda. You stay in the car till I take milk and bread. You must wait no matter how late.

I'm ready.

S.H, who has the hyena features was brown with big tusks, thin cheeks, unsteady walk. S.H knocked on the door, then a woman got out, he then followed her inside. She said to him: Come in, welcome:

He entered quickly and said to her: I brought milk and bread to you.

She replied: May God bless you.

He looked at her and felt embarrassed. Her features looked serious at first glance. He was afraid of her and confused, then he said: I'll bring more.

She said curtly. God will reward you.

He was not pleased with this situation, retreated, and got out and said to Omar: The situation was not good.

Why?

I was embarrassed.

How?

Her features were sharp.

This is the best.

I didn't understand

The easy woman is useless. I loved a woman in Tombouctou. I know how women think.

How did it go with her?

She was very tough, so I decided to kidnap her and escape to another city.

Did this happen?

No, the attempt failed.

How?

Her father came while I was about to get into the house, so I ran away from the whole area.

I came here.

Yes.

You then were arrested by the Polisario.

Yes, and I worked with them.

S.H laughed so hard and said: It is a good omen to have this happen. Without that, we would not have known you. Do you miss her?

Yes.

She might have married.

Sure, after all these years she probably got married.

So, you understand the meaning of love for a man.

Right.

Husniyya destroyed me.

Does she love you?

It is not necessary to love me.

But she is too young.

This is not important. We are everything here. Nobody can stand up to us.

Yes.

I have to get her and get this fool- Um Huda.

As for Um Huda it would be easy to get, but Hasania is a problem.

I beg you, don't say that. It won't calm me if I didn't take her back to the camp. Even if it cost me a fight. We fought battles and I will consider it one of the battles.

You are right. She is beautiful.

Chapter 8.

This time we are in a lemon field digging under the trees, cleaning the field, and harvesting lemon. We have known the lemon well. We had not seen a lemon tree in our life. Hmeid peeled a lemon, and supervisor Alsaleh came. He took it and threw it, reprimanding him, saying: The farmer will come and will raise hell if he sees us eating lemon.

He said that and left, then Hmeid said angrily: Are we prisoners to work in the lemon fields? We should eat.

Hmeid's personality began to be tough and strong after a year. After the supervisor had gone to another place, he took a full lemon and devoured it. He said: It is sour, but it has water.

I said to him: Lemon is useful.

While we were walking, a hard, sharp branch hit my head, and I started bleeding. Students came, then the supervisor took me to the nearby dispensary by the farmer's car. There was a nice female doctor who said to me: What happened to you?

The supervisor said: It is a branch of a tree.

I cried while blood was leaking from my head. I remembered mom and what she was doing now as the doctor was stitching the wound. We soon went back to the residence, and I was alone there trying to write a letter that won't reach my family. I wrote on the paper: I got hurt today, dad, there was heavy blood flow, and I found no one around. I feel sadness and alienation. Days pass dull and heavy; I come back exhausted every day from the fields. I couldn't even think. It is a lot of work. They use us in farming. We are workers now, and we are no longer students. Our life has become hell. I don't know how long we'll stay here. It is a tough life, and it is not a life of students.

I left the letter and tried to sleep but I couldn't, so I kept thinking about everything, but I didn't reach a result.

When evening came, Hmeid came back and said: I was worried about you and asked the supervisor to let me come back to help you, but he refused. How mean is this supervisor?

Never mind. I feel improvement. Everything is good. Don't worry.

Praise to Allah.

We slept early, we had to help the peasants the next day in coffee isolation. We are addicted to the coffee smell. We were drinking tea only. There was a peasant with us called Julio. He brought us some cheese sandwiches. This is the first time I tasted this cheese.

Hmeid said: This sandwich is tasty.

I nodded and said to him: Really?

We sat under the tree. The peasant was kind, he brought some tea to us, and then we went under the shade for a short time. It was hot. Hmeid said smiling: I want to have a farm.

I looked at him and said: What would we plant?

Everything.

You couldn't plant everything.

I like banana

I like sugar cane.

Hmeid was following an ant heading towards the shade. It seems that it was escaping from the sun. Hmeid said sadly and suddenly: What are they doing in the camp now? I wonder.

They'll be at home

They might go to school.

Yes.

And the families?

They are at home waiting for assistance.

Have you heard what they would give us for the work we do?

Yes

What would they give us?

Another student interrupted and said: They'll give us three pesos.

Hmeid said: What would you do with it?

I said to him: I don't know.

The student said: They offer eating and housing. We'll eat the sweets we see in the shops.

Hmeid said: I enjoy tasting those sweets.

I said to him: When you take money, buy something with it.

The student said: Would they allow us to go to the streets? We are as if in prison here.

I said to them: I think they would allow us when we grow up.

The student said happily: I got a letter from my family today.

Hmeid said, amazed: Really?

The student replied: Yes.

Hmeid said: I couldn't send anything, and I don't know what happened to my family.

I said: Me too, I didn't send anything.

Hmeid said: How did you send the letter?

The student said: Through a relative supervisor who helped me.

Hmeid said: What did they say to you in the letter?

The student said confidently: I'll get it out now. He put his hand into his pocket and got a folded letter.

He looked into it and said: They send greetings, and they say to me to take care of my health and pray.

Hmeid cried and said: I don't know anything about my family.

The student said: Never mind, life is as it is in the camp.

I said: Oh, God! Two years have passed since we came here.

The student said: Many years would pass. Time has no value. God knows if we would come back to the camp or not.

Hmeid said: I heard that we would come back at the end of the year.

I said, confirming: I also heard that. Ask your relative "Shall we come back to the camp or not?"

The student said: I will ask him, but don't tell anyone because he told me not to tell anyone.

I said to him: I won't tell anyone.

The peasant Julio came and got up to take care of the coffee trees, collect fruit, and put it in the sun. I felt exhausted suddenly due to the hot sun. The peasant noticed that and pointed to me to sit in the shade. The two stayed there working with the peasant who was uttering words we don't understand despite learning Spanish. In the afternoon we returned to have lunch and walked tiredly. Students were gathering around the kitchen's window. The supervisor was asking them to queue carrying their plates to put in rice and a piece of meat. We sat on the concrete bench, Hmeid and me and began eating rice greedily. We were hungry due to the chores we performed.

Hmeid said: When shall I eat chicken?

I said to him: On Wednesday, according to the schedule.

What about tomorrow, what should we have?

I think it's vegetables.

Hmeid said: I wish I could taste a piece of bread.

I said to him: Go to the cook and ask for it.

The supervisor will get angry.

No.

No, the supervisor will get angry.

Chapter 9.

My uncle and dad changed their place of residence in Azoki. Things got worse. My uncle decided to take a risk and visit an old friend in Laayoune camp, but my dad refused. My uncle responded, saying: If Ahmed had returned from Cuba, bring him rather than S.H takes him and tortures him. My dad was convinced by the idea. He was scared and was apprehensive about the idea.

My uncle rode his camel and got his rations and left for the Sahara with a piece of advice he had received from my dad, who is the knower of the secrets and problems of the Sahara.

The Sahara seemed to my uncle this time lonely. He left Kareem and Salma with us. He behaved as if he hadn't walked a meter before. And as if many eyes were monitoring him this time.

Oh, if this idiot man who doesn't follow the rules had got him alone. Is it plausible that this man remembers him after two years? He said to himself: I don't think so. As Salma, Kareem, Hasania and even my dad cried this time as they feared the unknown, and what awaits me if I returned to the camp. All heard that students would return back to see their families after years.

My dad said to mom: We were mistaken from the beginning. We crossed to Morocco where our families are, it would be better than this miserable life. You could care less about it.

My mom said: You are right; we haven't seen the good in the last two years.

You know what kept us here. Fatima. I miss Ahmed.

Mother tears and says: Me too.

She sobs and adds: I don't know what's happening with him now. Is he hungry or not?

Don't worry about him. Oh God, keep him away from bastards.

Is it believable that he had returned to the camp and didn't find us?

Maybe.

Where would he stay?

With neighbors, Abdulkareem's songs. They are decent and won't leave him for a moment.

Would he demand to stay with them? God forbids. I don't know how he would behave; I swear this is a catastrophe. He is a child.

Where would he go? Camp is camp.

It may be a rumor. Students come back after many years.

It it believable that they don't come back to their families after two years?

God knows. Time passes, and the game continues.

We are tired of moving in the Sahara. We want to rest in Morocco.

My mom said: We want Husniyya and Kareem to get married when your brother comes, and we go back to Morocco.

May God help them. I don't know how they would live this difficult life. Where did they go?

They went to the palm with sheep.

Water is scarce here.

When my brother comes back, we will depart for Morocco. He would have sent news to Ahmed that we were in Morocco.

It is their habit to keep people in camps and control them by kidnapping and detaining their sons.

At the nearby well, Husniyya, Salma and Kareem were taking out the water, and went back to shade. Hasania said: I wish Ahmed is with us now. We'll be happy.

Kareem replied encouraging: He'll come. His absence will not be long. I want to go to Morocco. Life here is meaningless.

Salma said smiling: In Morocco, there are cars, houses, streets, sea, fields, and a space of living, and here there is nothing except sand.

Kareem said: May god save my dad on this trip. I'm worried.

Husniyya said: Don't be afraid. Depends on God.

Salem said: I dreamt.

Kareem interrupted her quickly and said: What was your dream about?

Salma said: I dreamt that they caught him. This monster S.H caught him and tortured him, and he was calling out for our help.

Kareem replied: I'll kill him if he touches him.

Husniyya said: This man is a savage.

Kareem held sand and pressed it in his hand, and said: I won't leave him if he does something to my dad.

Husniyya said: It is just a dream. My uncle knows the Sahara and won't give up easily. He hates this man.

Salma said: May God make his affairs easy.

Kareem said: It would be a misery if my dad doesn't find Ahmed and turn out to be a rumor.

Salma said: Is it plausible?

Kareem said: Everything is possible.

Husniyya said with tears: I hope to God that Ahmed comes with my uncle , and then we leave for Morocco.

Kareem said, consoling: Don't worry, they will come together, and we'll leave the area.

Salma said: What is there in Cuba, Kareem?

Kareem said: As far as I know, Cuba is a far country where they study there.

Salma said: Ahmed wants to be a doctor; this is what he told me one day when we were young.

Hasania replied: That's right, he adores medicine. He is smart.

Kareem said: Oh God. Bring him back to us. He'll study medicine in Morocco, it is not a problem.

Husniyya smiled and said: And we'll get him to marry Salma.

Salma was ashamed, Kareem said laughing: She loves him.

Husniyya replied: She is shy.

Kareem said laughing: Yes.

The camps' sad streets where dogs have been messing with what they find of rubbish, were the only eyewitness on the grief of the miserable widow-Um Huda- whose S.H seemed nostalgic for her with previous experience as his way in sudden surprising love. Woe to those who refuse this experiment.

Um Huda thought deeply of this creature that began to harass her, and she didn't like his way of living. She thought of fleeing because he sent someone to ask her to go to his office in Alraboni for investigation since she didn't respond to his desires.

She arrived at the office in the morning, the guard told her to wait. S.H put his hands on his face and recalled many girls. No one stuck in his memory except for Um Huda and his wife who disgusted him with his life, and young Husniyya who fled, and he couldn't find her family who were disguised in Mauritania and no traces were found despite his many attempts till he finally gave up.

He pointed to the guard to let her come in and asked her to sit on the chair next to the door.

He asked her: How are you?

She said in grieve: The situation does not please anyone.

He said angrily: What do you mean?

She said challenging: What is there except hunger, destitute, illness and sand?

Do you ask?

No.

What did your husband die of?

I told you about that before.

I forgot.

Diabetes.

Didn't he find treatment?

Yes.

Treatment is available.

It is for you, not for him.

If you came and asked for it, we would find it for you, but the problem is that many people don't even know that there are foreign doctors of high level and with different specialties who treat people.

How will a human being live while his food is very bad, and water is impure?

It seems that we won't agree. I don't know what you are betting on here. Do you have anything in the camp? Nothing, so you must accept what is available.

What do you mean?

You know what I mean.

No, I don't know what you mean. I want you to tell me.

It seems we won't agree.

Do you think that I'm like those women who surrender to you just because you sent a bag of milk and sardine can?

I didn't mean that.

Then, what do you mean?

I mean, we need to get along.

I'm a widow. Look for a girl you could find everywhere.

Who told you that you didn't find one? There are many women.

So, what do you want from me?

I don't want anything. You could go back to your home easily.

Shall I get out?

Yes, I don't want to see your face. You are the loser.

Uncle Salem entered the Sahara borders, his heart was constricted. He didn't find anything to relieve and amuse him except singing. He arrived at AlSmara camp and went to neighbors to ask about me. They said that he had not come, and he might come next year.

He was disappointed, and he didn't wait. He just went to the heart of the Sahara, but he was surprised by a Polisario patrol that arrested him. They said that he was a spy and began interrogating him toughly. News reached S.H, who demanded to bring him to his office. He asked him: What brought you here?

My uncle said tiredly and weary: I came to look for my nephew.

Are you tired? Did they hit you?

Yes.

I will deal with you kindly if you tell me the truth.

Which truth?

Who sent you? Did Morocco send you?

No.

You are lying.

My nephew studies in Cuba.

What's his name?

Ahmed

Is he Ahmed Hassan?

Yes.

Then, you are one of Hassan's relatives, our neighbor in AlSmara camp.

Yes.

Where is your brother Hassan?

In Morocco.

Were you in Morocco with him?

No.

You lie.

I don't tell lies.

You'll pay a heavy price if you lie with any piece of information. Where did you come from?

I came from Mauritania.

What were you doing in Mauritania?

I came to see friends.

Do you have friends in Mauritania?

Yes.

Were you with your brother when you went to Mauritania?

Yes.

After that?

He went to Morocco, and I stayed in Mauritania.

Why didn't you go with him?

I prefer to stay in Mauritania in order to go back to the Sahara.

You lie. You were with your brother when I sent one of them to find out your location. I could help you if you helped me and told us the truth.

Which truth?

Where is your brother?

My brother is in Morocco.

In Morocco? Are you sure he is there? In which city?

In Dakhla.

Are you sure he is in Dakhla?

Yes.

Where is he exactly?

I don't know. He didn't tell me.

Are you sure of that? Doesn't he communicate with you?

No.

Where is your mobile?

I don't have one. I don't use it.

Why?

I never used it.

How can we be sure that your brother is in Dakhla?

Look for him.

Didn't he tell you which district he lives in?

No.

Did you marry his daughter Husniyya?

No.

Good.

There is much faulty information you present. Look at yourself. You'll die of torture, and you won't get except for loss. Be with me, and I'll help you. I'll build you a house and give you money if you agree and support me.

How?

I want to marry your niece Husniyya.

How can I help you?

I'll release you, and you bring her in one way or another or you give me information that leads me to her.

I have nothing to offer you. I said everything I had got.

You didn't tell the truth.

Believe me, I told the truth.

S.H looked outside, called the guard, and said to him: Relieve him of torture. He's a good man. Sure, he'll cooperate with me in the coming days.

The guard replied: Ok

He said, addressing my uncle: Next time we'll untie your feet. For whom are you subject to such torture? Think, Man, about yourself. If you don't cooperate with me, torture will be increased more. Do you understand what I say?

My uncle responded in a soft low voice: Yes.

S.H said to the guard: Bring a cup of water here.

The guard went and brought a cup of water, and then S.H added: Give him water.

The guard gave water to my uncle, who drank avariciously since he was thirsty. They had not given him water for long hours.

S.H said: Let them care for him in the cell and not torture him till we investigate his case. What happened to him is enough. If he didn't respond positively, then we know what we would do.

My uncle did not respond to S.H's demand to know more details, so he sent him to Alhafr. S.H had threatened to send him there. This Alhafr was the worst primitive and horrible jail. They used to put the Moroccan soldiers there. No one would believe that there are jails like this where they keep the prisoner. My uncle lived a very tough life in Alhafr.

They used to wake them up at three in the morning and hold cables, then hit them on their backs while they ran in the yard. There was no life in Alhafr but death. They ate the noodles and little soup, a small quantity that is hardly enough to suit a child. When they go outdoors, they go together to the Sahara. It was miserable; my uncle was severely depressed since he came from the width of the Sahara to the narrowness of this ditch. Two weeks later, he got a request. He went with the guard, and the car departed to Alraboni camp and left Tindouf. It was very hot, and S.H was waiting for him, and he said: How are things in Tindouf?

My uncle said angrily: Bad.

I told you, I don't like to send you there. Moroccan soldiers are tortured there, I don't like to be tortured with them.

My uncle was silent.

S.H said: Oh. Tell me. Would you stick to your contradicting information? You won't tell me where your brother, the dog, is, will you? I'll catch him.

My uncle said angrily: What do you want from him? What did he do?

S.H laughed hysterically and said: He did nothing, but I want to marry Husniyya.

My uncle said: Husniyya got married.

S.H said, shocked.

Got married?

Yes.

But you told me she did not marry.

Yes.

Then you are lying.

I don't lie. There are many women here, you could find one if you look.

I know what I want.

You want a very young girl.

This is my business.

You are free.

I'll get her at all costs; I'll not give up. Did you see how I found you after years? I didn't expect to find you face to face.

It was a mistake.

It is a strange world.

At this point, an idea came to his mind, and he decided to cheat him.

How sincere you are, man!

Really, I was sincere to my wife till she died of cancer, and I wanted to marry Husniyya.

Husniyya is not like that.

For whom, then?

You'll know when cables eat your back.

Why don't we have a deal?

About what?

I'll go and send Husniyya to you to get married.

It is a good idea, but how would you implement it?

I'll tell you later what is the advantage of my imprisonment in Tindouf. It is better that you get Husniyya.

What guarantee do I have that you are honest and will do it?

I'll tell you a plan that never fails.

I'll see.

Chapter 10.

We sometimes feel anxious and sad in our youth, a new year has just begun, which is the third year for us here in this country. We moved to another stage which is the harvest stage of sugar cane that starts the first month of the year. Each one held his cleaver, and our little hands started cutting sugar cane. I feel frustrated as I look at those fields. They are boundless. The sun burns us merciless l said to myself: Glory be Allah, we came from sand to the green area, but misery is misery. It doesn't change. If we had gone to a rich country for example. I heard that some students robbed a school in the neighborhood. We were lost in this country, we can no longer think. Where are you, dad? Where are you, mom? I looked at Hmeid, who took off his gloves because the sugar cane leaves were sharp.

I said to Hmeid: Where?

He said to me: The farmer demanded my help in making a sugar drink. They carried many sticks of sugar cane, cleaned them, and put them in a pot, then put it on fire, and then they completed the process of extracting the sweet syrup from the cane.

They put it in glass vessels and took it to the peasant's cottage. Hmeid came back, and I said to him: What is over there?

Hmeid said: He is putting it in a cold place.

I said to him: He won't give us a drink, will he?

It is hot, it needs to cool off.

Hmeid put his gloves on, the peasant who asked us to carry the sticks to a small yard near the cottage came, so the sticks began to gather because the car will come in the afternoon. All the products will be taken to the nearby factory.

Hmeid said sarcastically: We produce sugar, and we don't see it but for a short time.

I said to him: I don't like sugar.

He replied angrily: Is there anyone who doesn't like sugar? I remember we drank tea with dad. How delicious is the tea of the camp?

You reminded me of my dad when we drank tea as we were taking care of the sheep in the Sahara and chanting. How beautiful those days were!

Those days won't return. I feel that those days won't return.

God knows when we'll go back to the camp. Now the third year has started.

I said smiling: We'll never come back. It seems that we'll stay in this country forever.

I heard the supervisor saying that a group of Cuban doctors would go to the camps.

What are they doing there? People don't need doctors, they need everything.

The go-to practice for people.

Doctors here are strong. There aren't any doctors in the camps.

I laughed and said: A country from one camp?

Hmeid said, whispering: A student has arrived. Lower your voice. A student talked about the Polisario and was punished, we are tired without punishment.

I said to Hmeid as a pun: I love Cuban cigars.

Hmeid replied: I wish I smoked a cigarette. It seems golden and beautiful.

The student has gone, so Hmeid said: Well done, this boy is a spy.

I know.

How did you know?

He gets up at night to see the supervisor and tell him about what the students had said.

Oh God. Even here we have spies.

Yes.

I heard the supervisor talking with an elderly Sahrawi who works at another school. He was telling him that they deceived the prisoners here by bringing false women who pretended they were journalists and asking about the conditions in prison. When answers are unsatisfactory, they torture them.

Sure, they speak many languages.

That's right, to cheat prisoners.

They are specialized in espionage.

Sure

It is a sad thing.

I heard him saying to his friend they found more than a girl who engages in prostitution with Cuban gangs, and they didn't do anything.

It is a tragedy that they sell us everywhere in turn for trivial things.

Yes, I heard they sell kids in lieu of aids in many countries and even for gangs.

Oh God, for gangs!

Yes.

We'll grow up here. I began to forget the Arabic Language, and I forgot everything.

We won't forget.

We won't forget our family at any cost.

Sure.

My friends in Spain sold them to many families.

What is this curse upon us?

God is examining us. They take children and transport them to Cuba to work on farms and train on weapons. What country sells its children, boys and girls, if they were from the Sahrawi sons.

Many might have gone there. They are not from that area. They are disgruntled Africans, and Cubans, and others exercise interrogation and torture people.

But we must work hard to go to the university at least.

You are right.

Failed return to the camps will be a disaster.

We must leave Camaguey.

I hate this city.

Me too.

It reminds me of the slaves whom they brought from Africa.

Right. They brought the African here to work in fields. Now they bring us to work on farms once again. We are sons of the Sahara; we come here to work on farms.

It is forced labor.

Everything around us, Hmeid and I, encourages us to work hard to reach the university. I used to visit Thomas and Orinda on the weekend. They were an old couple with no children. They were sympathetic to me, and we got some crumbs and gave it to them. They felt happiness.

Thomas said to me: How do you feel after spending many years in Cuba?

I said to him: It's OK.

Orinda said: Do you miss your parents?

I said to her sadly: Yes.

She said tenderly as she was going to the kitchen: Do you like rice and beef?

I answered: Yes.

Thomas said, laughing: Ahmed likes your food, Orinda.

Orinda said smiling: If I had a daughter, I would have her married to you, Ahmed, you are hardworking, I saw your school certificate.

I felt confident and said to her:

I want to become a doctor.

Thomas said: Cuba has become famous for teaching medicine. The world comes here to learn.

Orinda said: Excuse me; I want to go to the kitchen.

I said to her: Shall I come to help you?

She replied: No.

Thomas said: If you want to work, clean the garden of leaves, and come back to talk and tell me about the Sahara.

Despite poverty, their humble house in Camaguey seemed happy and beautiful. They plant lemon and citrus, and keep a dog called Jolly. I didn't get along with this dog. He used to bark when he saw me, till he began to be familiar with me at the end when I offered him beef while he was tied. I cleaned the garden. An hour later, Thomas looked out the window and called me. Their house was wooden and simple. He arrived and sat; he was drinking tea in front of the house. I sat with him. He said: Work never ends, come and drink tea, you love it.

He added: How is your family?

I said to him: I don't know anything about them.

He said angrily: How tough are these guys, they don't allow you to communicate with your families?!

This is what has happened.

You'll be a famous doctor and then you return back to them.

God willing.

Chapter 11.

My uncle was there for more than a month, my dad was worried, news arrived that he was arrested so he decided to escape to Morocco. In fact, this is what had happened, and he went to Tan-Tan after he had sold his sheep and his brother's sheep. He got Kareem to marry Husniyya without ceremony, then he rented a house in the city and started looking for a job till he found it in one of the fish factories. Kareem worked with him. Another month passed and my dad was waiting for his brother who never came.

One night, Kareem was addressing my dad: What will you do, uncle?

My dad said: Allah is my best deputy, what can we do?

I want to look for my dad.

My dad said quickly: What are you saying, Kareem? We were mistaken when we sent your dad. Do you want us to repeat the mistake? And then you fall in the hands of the Polisario, which are merciless.

Husniyya said: We should think about what we shall do.

My mom replied: No one will go there, they will drag everyone, and they won't leave anyone.

Kareem said: What shall we do?

My dad replied: We'll do nothing.

Salma said: You should rest from work, uncle. I want to work.

My dad said: May God bless you, daughter. This work won't bother me.

My mom replied, laughing: Don't worry about him. I want to buy some sheep and depart this city, it is better.

My dad looked at her and said: This is a sensible idea.

Kareem said: How could we reach the work?

My dad said: We'll keep this house, but we'll return to the nearby Sahara with sheep and move between them.

Husniyya replied: It is a good idea

Months passed through give- and – take debate between my uncle, Salem, and S.H who asked the guard to go on torturing my uncle more and more, and at the end of each month, they take him to Alraboni in an attempt to find out how far is he ready to talk about Hasania's location. This time, S.H was very angry and said to my uncle: What do you have this time?

My uncle replied, weary: I have a lot.

Did you come to tell me something this time?

My uncle looked exhausted and sick: Yes.

Where is Husniyya?

I'll tell you.

What would you tell me?

Would you take me out from here?

Yes.

When?

As soon as you tell me.

Really, she is there in Azoki.

Are you sure?

Yes.

How can I believe that?

I swear.

It seems you are tired.

Yes, I'll die.

No, man. We need you.

I can't. I'm afraid of death.

Never mind. I'll ask them to alleviate the torture till we confirm the validity of what you say.

I don't want to be sure. I came from there.

I believe you but are there for a while. I'm afraid they have left the area when you have been gone all this time.

They won't leave me.

You don't know. We'll be sure.

He asked the guard to take my uncle out. He met a Spanish delegation and talked about fake tournaments. And many needs while his son was studying in Madrid.

He called Omar after the delegation had departed and said to him:

What appointments do we have today?

I summoned um Huda yesterday.

Right? Bring her, please.

Um Huda came. She was in prison while they sent her daughter to study in Cuba.

S.H laughed and said to her: If you agreed to work with me, you wouldn't be in prison now, you trivial woman.

He added: Why are you silent?

She replied heartbroken: What could I say?

Say anything.

I'll say to you that I'll never accept you even if there are no men.

You are going too far.

You deserve that.

I won't hit you now. I let the guard hit and rape you. As for me, I won't defile my hands with you.

You are defiled.

You'll see in the prison things you had never experienced before, you –the Moroccan spy.

I don't know Morocco.

How come? Whoever hates the revolution, and the revolutionaries is a Moroccan spy.

Morocco is better than you.

Damn you.

Chapter 12.

I said to Thomas: I want to stay in Cuba. I don't want to come back to work with these monsters.

Orinda said: What are they doing there?

I said to her: They sell children in lieu of milk, sugar and sardine.

Thomas said astonished: Is this possible?

I replied: They send them to Spain and other countries for adoption in exchange they get money. They bring them to Cuba for the purpose of getting the aids they steal.

Orinda said: Then, you should stay in Cuba.

Thomas said: But the state may get angry.

Orinda said: Ahmed will stay with us.

Thomas replied: It is still early. He will study at the university, and then we don't know what will happen.

I said to Thomas: My marks are high, so I'll study medicine.

Orinda said: This is great.

My days were not all beautiful. Hmeid was sick, but he recovered from fever, and got a high score, which pleased me. We began exploring together at night the streets of Camaguey.

I said to Hmeid: I see that you are staggering. What's the matter with you? We are on the street.

Hmeid replied heavily:

I drank.

Damn you. When did you drink?

Bilal brought whiskey and we drank.

You got mad. We agreed to stay true to our religion.

I felt bored and said let me change a little bit. I'm bored, man.

O.K. Drink a cup of coffee.

We went back to our residence, and she made a cup of coffee for Hmeid. He drank and went back to his senses. He said laughing:

I didn't drink much.

How much did you drink?

Half a small cup.

I laughed so hard and said to him:

You get drunk on smell.

S.H sent an armed group to Azoki to explore the area. Indeed, local residents said that the group was here but departed, and they didn't know the destination, so they went back to Alraboni and told S.H about what had happened to them. He hurried and summoned my uncle Salem and said: We went to Azoki, and we didn't find anyone there.

My uncle responded: I told you the truth.

S.H said angrily: Listen to me, man, you didn't look at yourself in the mirror. You lost weight; you'll die soon if you don't tell the truth.

My uncle said sadly: I told the truth.

No, you didn't tell the truth. We went to Azoki and asked there but we found no trace of them. You know where they had gone.

Believe me, I don't know where they had gone

And I say to you will stay imprisoned in Alhofra until death.

My uncle said crying: You promise to release me.

You won't get out; you'll die here, bastard.

My uncle went crying, his heart was weak, and he couldn't bear this torment. He said to Kamal-the prisoner next to him: It seems I'll stay here. This dog- called S.H will not release me.

The guard brought the noodles, pot, and the prisoners started cooking it on fire. Everyone ate, their bodies began to break down. It is a very difficult life there. They torture them in primitive ways.

Kamal-the Moroccan prisoner soldier, said: What do you think of escaping?

My uncle agreed, and they began planning, but escaping was not that easy in Tindouf.

Kamal said: How can we start?

My uncle replied: Let's think of the cuffs on our hands.

No. we should think of cuffs on our legs because cuffs on the hands are easy.

This is Tindouf, and it is desert. How could we escape?

We should think.

But they stand with their guns, not far away.

We should benefit from the darkness.

Darkness is a good idea.

They don't leave us for a moment. What should we do? Let's think quietly.

Do you know, Kamal, I know the desert well. I hope to be in it. They wouldn't know where I had gone.

We'll die of thirst.

I know where wells are.

Do you know the entire desert?

Yes.

I hope so.

I often walked in the desert. I moved in it in length and breadth. I don't think it will give up on me. These are mercenaries and know nothing.

I hope the day I go back to Morocco. I didn't expect to see and suffer all this torment.

I heard the Red Cross would come.

Impossible, the Red Cross won't come here and see people in Alhafr as the primitive man without food or anything.

Where would the Red Cross go?

Maybe to a better prison than these strange prisons.

I don't believe that there are prisons in the world like these prisons.

Even in war, they don't know its principles.

Certainly, they are not its cavalry. We deal with them respectfully in Morocco.

Think quietly to be able to escape.

I'll think about it. I was an officer.

Yes.

Despite the difficult situation.

You'll not stay here forever. I feel terrified when I think of that.

You are right. Hitler did not do that with prisoners. Is it believable there are human beings who think that way?

Take it easy. We'll get out. Just thinking of that means to be on the road.

Oh God!

Husniyya gave birth to a boy, and my dad named him Salem despite the objection of Salma, but my dad said: It is OK to call the name of brave men more than one time.

He looked like my uncle Salem, but he was beautiful and had a light tan, soft skin and beautiful eyes. He got beauty from Hasania, and strength from Kareem. Salma cried and said: Where is dad, to see his grandson?

My dad said confidently: Your father will come. Depending on God, his absence will not be long.

My mom said: He'll come one day.

Salma cried, my dad said: We all know, there is no need to remind us with this matter.

Salma said: God will not forget him.

Husniyya said: My uncle is a brave man, he'll endure.

Salma said crying: I don't know how long?

My mother said: Depends on God.

My dad said: What will you do for us, Kareem? We want Tagine.

My mom said smiling: No, we need Couscous.

Husniyya said: We'll cook couscous with vegetables for you.

Kareem replied:We'll eat meat. Salem deserves that we celebrate him.

My dad said: We'll slaughter a sheep to celebrate this occasion. Our lives have become sad.

Kareem said: So, on Friday evening you'll slaughter a sheep, uncle.

Yes, Friday evening.

The little enfant cried, Salma who was attached to her dad cried with him, she remembered how he was carrying her when she was young.

We didn't rest and have peace of mind on this island. Strong blows on this island. Supervisor Alsaleh said: Everyone should prepare the windows. They distributed some hammers, and nails, then we started closing windows and placing some panels on the windows.

Hmeid said: What is going on?

A student said: A tornado comes tonight.

Another student said: What is a tornado?

The first one said: Strong wind.

Hmeid said: What are these preparations for?

I said to Hmeid: He is uprooting everything.

Hmeid asked: How?

Oh. His strength is horrible. It uproots trees and destroys everything.

A student said: Will it destroy the building on our heads?

I said to him: No.

We went to the dormitory, supervisor Alsaleh passed by and said: Put off the lights.

A light was still coming from his room.

Sound of the wind was howling horribly. We began hearing the horns of the ambulance and the police.

Hmeid said horrified: What's over there?

I said: The hurricane has intensified. Listen! It is hitting the window. The sound of raindrops caused a strong crack.

The nearby by student said: What would happen? It is a horrible hurricane and is stronger than the previous year.

Hmeid said: Really.

Another student said: It is called Gustav Hurricane. It is strong and will destroy houses if it keeps the same speed.

A student who came from the corridor said: It is approaching the beach. Waves will rise and cities will drown.

I said quickly: We should be careful.

The supervisor entered quickly and lit the ward, and said: Tomorrow is a holiday. You stay in your positions, and you are not allowed to get out of the ward, you'll receive instructions. Then he left in a hurry.

Hmeid said: Everything is beautiful here except hurricanes.

Another student said: What is nice here? Nothing nice here. I wish I went to the Sahara.

A nearby student said: Life here is more beautiful.

Hmeid said sarcastically: Where is beauty? In the morning, we work in fields and in the evening we study. It is a catastrophe. I wish I didn't come here.

The student replied: There is nothing in the Sahara except sand.

Another one said: I wish it was so and was limited to sand. Things are worse with these thugs who steal everything and sell children in lieu of the aid that does not reach them.

I said to them: Please be silent in case one of them goes and tells the supervisor.

I haven't finished yet until the supervisor entered and lit fire and said: The dogs that attack the revolution should be punished.

One of the students entered and pointed to Hmeid and another student. The supervisor took them to the third floor, and they were hit on their feet until their feet were swollen, then they were taken to the ward crying.

The supervisor said: The fate of everyone who attacks the revolution will be like those dogs. Anyone who tells the Cubans what had happened would only get torture and beating.

Hmeid kept crying with swollen legs. They used to bring hot water and salt to conceal the marks of beating.

The surprise was that the headmistress came and wrote an official complaint against the supervisor and the man who is in charge of the Polisario who was reprimanded. She demanded from the Polisario to replace him due to his irregularities and infringements against young students. Hmeid was taken to a nearby dispensary to be medicated.

The situation was getting more tense with the supervisor – Alsaleh. The headmistress decided that he will not work with this ward and was transferred. I stayed close to Hmeid, helping him by the request of the new supervisor.

Hmeid said crying: I want to talk to dad.

I said to him I will tell the supervisor. When the new supervisor came, I told him. He didn't say anything. I told the headmistress who demanded the same, but she didn't respond.

I said to Hmeid: We have to be patient for a few years, and everything will end, then we go to another place.

Hmeid said: Where should we go?

I said to him: We'll go to Nicaragua.

Where is Nicaragua?

It is near here. We won't go to the Sahara to find the Polisario.

It is the best solution.

We'll live there then we go back to Morocco.

How can we find our families?

We'll find them. It is not a problem. We'll go to Morocco and know everything.

It's a reasonable idea.

And we'll bring them to live with us in Morocco. It is undermining man and his dignity in the misery camps.

Our life was lost.

No, it was not lost. We'll start again –God willing. We will be doctors and help our families in Morocco.

Will Morocco accept us?

Sure. I know many stories like these. Morocco is a merciful country.

Days will pass as usual, and the year is 2002, S.H will stay roaming in deception. During that time, my uncle Salem died affected by the pain he felt due to those wounds he sustained while escaping. Nobody will know anything about him.

Little by little, this matter was revealed, and my dad had a stroke and he died sadly. He complains also from the injustice of S.H who spends his life chasing girls from time to time and continues his path. Um Huda won't be his last victim who was suddenly assassinated and was buried quietly as a patient who died in prison.

At the end, he had a heart attack and died, and hundreds of tales about the embezzlement of aids and funds died with him. Moreover, many women's adventures died as well. My dad and uncle, similarly, will die seeking rest but they'll find it. These militias made their lives unbearable. They were just hell, just two leaves of the Sahara tree that fall due to the absurdity of these persons.

My mom cried in a way she had never cried before and said: We were displaced by those. They stole my son, killed many people from our family. then she said to Kareem: How could we find Ahmed after all this time?

Chapter 13.

At the end of my study at Camaguey university, Hmeid and I would agree to escape to Nicaragua when the plane landed there. This is what happened, and we are now in Pasaya. We'll work at a hospital in the capital, and arrange our conditions little by little, then we'll get used to life in Nicaragua.

Later, I'll get married to Orinda and settle in a new house in the capital as Hmeid stays in Pasaya and gets married as well to a girl called Alma. We limit our stay in Nicaragua to one year only before we agree to travel to Morocco. We are now at Mohammed V Airport in Casablanca heading towards Laayoune to reside and work there. We'll put our photos on facebook and ask for friends to help us find our families or get any information about them. Soon, I found out that my family is in Morocco through my sister Hasania's page. Our meeting in Tan-Tan will be touching as well as the attempt of recalling our lost years of life. My mom will ask me to work in Tan-Tan, but I'll tell her that I work in Laayoune, then Kareem will slaughter a sheep for me and Orinda- my wife-. After that I'll visit my dad's tomb, and Orinda says to me that she liked life in the Sahara. I told that to my mother.

My mom couldn't believe what she saw. She didn't expect to see me once again. Children killed in Cuba, lost girls, and everything was done for the sake of getting aids.

Still the series of exporting children exists. As for Hmeid, he still hasn't found his parents. He sent many letters hoping that one came from a camp with news about his parents.

Many families were destroyed and disintegrated. Children migrated and children were sold, and others changed their religion according to the new parents. It is a systematic destruction for those dwelling as prisoners in Tindouf where they could not leave. They are in great distress and humiliating detention.

Alpha Book Publisher

Made in the USA
Columbia, SC
20 December 2022